It is only fitting that we should begin this series with what we consider to be absolutely and without exception the greatest single exercise known to man, for conditioning the entire body, improving the health and energy, strengthening the function of the internal organs, giving the most rapid gains in bodyweight, adding to all around athletic ability. That is quite a large order but we feel that it is very true and we could add a lot more claims for this exercise. In addition to this, I feel I could write a book just about this one exercise, its performance and results. (Rader, 1955a, p. 22)

—Peary Rader
Founder of *Iron Man* magazine
Publisher and Editor 1936–1986

"Are squats the key exercise in this routine?" Eddie asked him.

"Squats are the key exercise in any routine," the gym owner said. "Your gains will be roughly proportionate to the effort you put into squatting. The heavier you squat the more you'll gain, and without them you won't gain at all." (McCallum, 1971, p. 78)

We can sum up the essentials very quickly. Squats and milk. That's the gist of it. Heavy squats and lots of milk and never mind if the principle is twenty years old.

If you're in doubt, let me tell you this. I get scores of letters from lifters around the country who've tried the squats and milk program. They all say the same thing. They gained more weight in a month on the squats and milk than they had in a year or more on other types of programs. Gains of twenty to thirty pounds in a month are not uncommon. If you don't gain at least ten pounds a month you're doing something wrong. (McCallum, 1968b, p. 13)

SUPER
SQUATS

SUPER
SQUATS

HOW TO GAIN

30 POUNDS OF MUSCLE

IN 6 WEEKS

By Randall J. Strossen, Ph.D.

IronMind® Enterprises, Inc.
Nevada City, California

"Stronger minds, stronger bodies."

Super Squats was written with the intention of increasing your well-being. But just as when you cross the street, you follow this program solely at your own risk. Check with your physician before beginning this or any other exercise program.

First printing: April 1989
Second printing: September 1989
Third printing: October 1990
Fourth printing: January 1992
Fifth printing: October 1992
Copyright © 1989 by Randall J. Strossen, Ph.D.

ISBN: 0-926888-00-5

Printed in the United States of America

Acknowledgments

Many thanks to Messrs. James E. Douglass, Andrew W. Jackson, John C. Grimek, Fred R. Howell, Joe Roark, Charles A. Smith, and Chester O. Teegarden, as well as to Dr. Terry Todd, for helping me research an essential element of this book: Joseph Curtis Hise. Make no mistake about it, J. C. Hise is the central character in this story and he would have gotten short shrift without the generous help of these Iron Game historians. A particularly deep debt on this score is owed to Mr. James E. Douglass, of Monticello, Utah, who provided the vast majority of my education on his very good friend, "Lil Yosie."

Dedication

This book is dedicated to the memories of Mark Hamilton Berry and Joseph Curtis Hisc, who blazed much of the trail we are going to follow, and to Peary Rader and John McCallum for upholding this tradition and teaching me most of what I know of value about training with weights.

Contents

A Note to Readers

If you are extremely impatient to start on this program, chapter 1 alone will probably give you enough information to begin reaping its benefits. History buffs, the show-me-some-proof-crowd, and the just-plain-curious-types will definitely want to read chapter 2, even if others might simply choose to skip it. Chapters 3 and 4 give you all the nuts and bolts of the program, with sufficient detail to put you, fully armed, on the road to a stronger, more muscular body. Chapter 5 addresses some of the finer points of the program and takes you well beyond the basics in several key areas.

This book talks expressly about men, and we consistently use male referents throughout this book because we are drawing from a history of men who developed and applied these techniques. However, women can easily benefit by applying the program just as men would—gaining weight, increasing their strength, and improving their health. Also, in terms of body shaping, this program can probably rival *anything* available for women who would like to increase the arch of their chests and the curve of their derrières. The bottom line here is that women should get under the squat bar and build a little history of their own by transforming themselves, just as men have been doing for over half a century.

Some readers might not be used to reading fully referenced books, books that tell you exactly where to find the original material underlying any particular statement made by the author. *Super Squats* is presented in this style for a variety of reasons, but you need not give the references a second thought if they bother you. On the other hand, if you are intrigued by a particular topic, or dispute the accuracy of a claim, having a fully documented text in your hand will make it easy to carry out any related research projects you would like to pursue. Even if you never go back to a single original citation, the thoroughly documented nature of this book should help convince even the most skeptical reader that this program really has proven its worth again and again—rather than just being another fleeting fashion manufactured by a self-proclaimed trainer of champions.

Foreword

You are about to encounter a program for getting big and strong that is so effective it can stand up to anything going. Absolutely anything. Yet this program is so straightforward that you will probably wonder why you haven't heard about it before—especially because the claims made for it, while truthful, are so utterly fabulous.

Twenty-five years ago it was already noted that the classic 20-rep squat programs were seldom used anymore, despite the "fantastic gains" they produced (Kallos, 1963, p. 16). This trend was explained by a current preference for exercises that isolated individual muscles, as well as by noting that the 20-rep squat programs were awfully hard work. These reasons help explain today's continued low profile of this unparalleled method for getting big and strong, but the root cause is found far from the gym—in the land of economics.

Muscles and strength have become big business: contests, supplements, equipment, magazines, clothing. Entire industries flourish where a few short years ago none existed or a couple struggled. These businesses need to have something of perceived value, something unique that others will pay for, ideally again and again. From the standpoint of personal economic gain the 20-rep squat program is a lightweight, because there's really almost nothing to sell—no need for secret routines, fancy equipment, chemical enhancers, or exotic supplements.

Even the most brilliant marketers in muscledom are un-
likely ever to make a bundle on this program; worse yet, if
everyone started using this program, it could put a dent in
their existing sales. If you can gain twenty to thirty pounds
of real muscle in a few weeks, using ordinary food and
common equipment, why would you spend a fortune on
their latest gimmicks? You probably wouldn't.

Of course, our psychological processes being what they
are, you might not be inclined to believe the claims made
of this program simply because there really is nothing for
you to buy. In fact, the original creative genius who applied this program—Joseph Curtis Hise—ran smack into
this wall half a century ago. Some people refused to believe
him, "especially since we only tried to give them good advice instead of trying to sell them something" (Berry,
1933c, p. 17). Don't assume that you won't have to pay
your dues on this program, however, because it carries a
price tag marked in the currency of very hard work and the
underlying will to succeed.

This program is a classic with immense current value.
One of the most highly regarded current bodybuilding authors has noted that even though you never hear much
about breathing squats these days, they are tremendously
effective and packed "a full six inches" on his chest in his
first year of training (Brainum, 1988, p. 113). Given their
incredible ability to stimulate growth, squats have recently
been dubbed "the natural maxibolic" (Coyle, 1988, p. 62)
and are about to be rediscovered.

Let's not forget that Arnold Schwarzenegger built his
foundation on bench presses and squats, following in the
footsteps of his hero, the Herculean Reg Park (Schwarzenegger and Hall, 1979). And Reg Park, who was always a
strength athlete among many mere bodybuilders, laid his
foundation by doing 20-rep squats with over 300 pounds
during his building-up phase (Zeller, 1988). How about
Tom Platz? "You must squat to achieve your full body-

building potential ... it's a total body exercise" (Charles, 1988, p. 37). Dean Tornabene certainly has access to all the whiz-bang programs kicking around today, so what does he say?

> The squat is a giant stimulus — not only for the legs but for other parts of the body, too. I often say that if I were thrown in jail and I was allowed to weight train only half an hour three times a week, I would just do squats. That's it. (Charles, 1988, p. 37)

And finding a lifter today who doesn't know the value of heavy squatting is probably harder than finding gold in your closet. So don't worry, the magic of heavy squats works as well now as it did fifty years ago, whether you're in a small midwestern town or Santa Monica, California.

Follow this program for at least six weeks and drop me a line, if you like, letting me know just how much progress you made. Until then, think positively, squat hard and heavy, eat a lot of good food, drink gallons of milk, and start saving for a new wardrobe. Good luck!

Randall J. Strossen, Ph.D.
President
IronMind® Enterprises, Inc.
P.O. Box 1228
Nevada City, CA 95959

1 Bulging with Basics: Introducing 20-Rep Squats

Veteran gym rats aside, chances are good you have never heard about one of the most effective ways to build muscular size and strength, no matter how much chrome you have pumped in gyms that look like medical clinics or fern bars. That's because muscledom's marketers hawk personal trainers, designer sweats, da Vincian equipment, convoluted routines, mega supplements, and name brand gyms—they sell a ton of sizzle for each ounce of the steak you want. Before the next time you lace up your Reeboks, consider getting big and strong by lifting weights the old fashioned way.

Half a century ago, a decade before Arnold was born, the pioneers of the Iron Game had equipment that was crude by today's standards and none of the food supplements or drugs that have spawned the current crop of bodybuilding and lifting champions. Nonetheless, these hardy souls developed a system virtually guaranteed to pile muscular bulk on even the frailest physique, a system that works as well today as it did then.

Men who had been unable to register significant gains with other routines were suddenly gaining twenty pounds of muscle in a month or two. If you have trouble visualizing these results in bodybuilding terms, look at twenty pounds of lean beef in the butcher shop and picture that much mass added to your chest, shoulders, arms, back, and legs. That sort of progress turns befores into afters, transforming proverbial ninety-eight pound weaklings into hunks who no longer have to worry about getting sand kicked in their faces. The system that produces these results is simple, but not easy. It builds real muscle, increases one's strength enormously, and gives the cardiovascular system something more than a tickle in the process. About the only drawback to following this routine is that you will outgrow your clothes.

The nucleus of this venerable program is one set of squats—twenty reps in the set, to be sure, but just one set. Additional exercises are incidental, two or three sets of several other basic exercises at most, and the general caution is to err on the side of doing too few additional exercises rather than too many. With one set of squats plus a couple of sets of bench presses and bent over rows as the prototypical routine, these workouts hardly compare to the half-day affairs common to today's bodybuilding and lifting stars or to what's hyped in the glossy muscle magazines. Make no mistake about it, however, this one set of 20-rep squats is not your ordinary cup of iron tea: Whatever our recipe might lack in complexity or volume will be more than recouped in intensity.

In addition to the 20-rep squats, trainees are advised to eat a lot of wholesome food, drink at least two quarts of milk a day, and to get plenty of rest in between the twice- or thrice-weekly workouts. That's it: one set of 20-rep squats, a couple of other basic exercises, plenty of good food, milk, and rest. But, oh, those squats!

The specific approach to the 20-rep squats is nearly as simple as the overall program. First, load the bar to what you normally use for ten reps. Now, do twenty reps—no kidding. Second, every single workout, add at least five pounds to the bar. These two elements are what separate the men from the boys and produce results, by simultaneously embracing the two cardinal principles of weight training: overload and progressive resistance.

The overload principle states that unless you do more than you are used to, you won't build muscular size or strength. All those training clichés like "no pain, no gain" reflect the overload principle. By requiring twenty reps with your normal ten-rep poundage, you are forced into overload mode. The principle of progressive resistance goes back to Milo of Crotona, who carried a calf a given distance each day in ancient Greece—as the calf grew, so did Milo, getting bigger and stronger for his efforts. Adding five or ten pounds to your squat bar every workout simulates the process of carrying a growing calf and most people, urbanites especially, find it more convenient.

Back to the squats. Load the bar to your normal ten-rep poundage, wrap a towel around it to give your upper back and shoulders a little padding, step under the bar, lift it off the squat racks, back up one step, force in two or three deep breaths, and knock off the first rep. Nothing fancy here, just a conventional deep knee bend, squatting down until the tops of your thighs are parallel to the floor and then coming back up. By the fifth rep, you should be fully warmed up, squatting smoothly, and the deep breathing should be coming naturally.

After the tenth rep, your body is done and your mind becomes the vehicle that either moves or stalls in the face of the challenge to reach the twentieth rep. At least three deep breaths, lots of positive self-instruction ("Come on, baby," "You can do it," "Down and up," "Puuush"), and the eleventh rep is history. More of the same for another rep or two and then the breathing and psyching become more serious. Maybe five to ten lung-bursting breaths in between each rep, your mind humming at psychedelic levels and your demeanor ferocious as a Ninja warrior, get you up to rep number fifteen. Now the game changes again because not only do the breathing and the pep talks become still more important, but each squat becomes an event performed in a dilated-time capsule where you, as you, fade, becoming more of an observer than an actor. If your mind falters, you are dead meat now, so you either get tough and grow, or cave in and stay small.

By rep number sixteen the bar cuts deeply into your back and mashes your entire body into the floor, giving you a new sense of appreciation for Newton's analyses of gravity. Your breathing sounds like a steam engine and your legs are probably starting to shake. Sheer willpower is the only way to make that rep. You remember that everything else was just a warm-up for the last several reps—they're the ones that make you grow—and you are blind to everything but the pattern: breathe, squat, rise. By the time you finish the eighteenth rep, you are guaranteed of completing the set if you psyched up properly beforehand, because what has become the most important thing in the world to you—knocking off those twenty reps—is within sight. It doesn't matter if each of those last two reps takes ten deep breaths, drives you berserk, leaves you purple-faced and quivering as you fight your way back up, through the sticking point of each squat: You are not going to be denied your victory.

When you complete the twentieth rep and manage to get the bar back on the squat racks, reeling with fatigue-induced delirium, you collapse on a bench for a set of light pullovers to stretch your rib cage, expanding the framework for the slabs of muscle you are adding to your upper body.

After the squats and pullovers are done, you might pass out, puke, think you have gone over the edge, or be incapable of walking up or down a flight of stairs to save your life—but get some rest, drink your milk, and go back at it in two or three days. The same thing all over again, but with five more pounds.

No wimps allowed in this program, but the fanatical fringe who can follow the regimen are assured, no matter how wispy their origins, of getting bigger and stronger than they ever dreamed possible. All that without any Lycra, Dianabol, Nautilus, or branched-chain amino acid supplements. Just twenty reps of squats, milk, sleep, and the will to demonstrate, under the bar, that mind over matter is more than just a clever little saying.

2 The Master Exercise in Perspective: A Brief History of Squats

Because of all the wonderful things they do, squats are worth discussing, and there's no better way to gain an appreciation for them than to review a little of their history. You'll soon understand why squats are—without question—the premiere exercise, regardless of whether you are primarily interested in improving your physique, your strength, your health, or all three.

To start off, when you think of building up your body, chances are good that you visualize bigger, stronger arms and shoulders, a more massive, powerful chest—not big legs. So why all this talk about squats? This paradox was unraveled over half a century ago:

> Experience has proven beyond any doubt that the most certain means of expanding the chest is through the medium of strenuous leg exercise, and it has likewise been the experience of those who have tried out this theory that improvement of the shoulders and arms will in time follow when the standard of the legs and torso has been raised. (Berry, 1933b, p. 17)

To be blunt, heavy leg work is the fastest route to big arms, shoulders, and chests.

If it's starting to sound like squats resemble a magic wand of sorts, that's because, properly employed, their powers for rendering positive physical transformations are more awesome than anything else going. As with most things that work, the highly effective squat programs available today are the result of years of experimentation and refinement. In fact, if you want to get specific and talk about hardcore research and bedrock empirical evidence for how to best build bulk and power, the *Super Squats* program has all others beaten hands down.

Up to the early 1920s Americans did squats up on their toes, which necessitated using fairly light weights, and the exercise hadn't yet achieved the special status it would when the German immigrant Henry "Milo" Steinborn introduced his new homeland to the practice of doing very heavy flat-footed squats (Paschall, 1954b). Henry Steinborn had begun training during World War I, while in an Australian concentration camp. He went on to win the German heavyweight lifting championship in 1920, and emigrated to the United States the next year (Klein, 1964). Among Steinborn's feats was his often-cited ability to up end a 550-pound barbell, rock it into position on his shoulders, do a squat, and return it in the same fashion! As impressive as this feat was in itself, its real impact might have come from the fact that Steinborn was a star in the quick lifts—capable of near world records in the snatch and the clean and jerk—and this ability was derived mainly from his great leg strength (Willoughby, 1981). Further vital evidence of the benefits of heavy squatting is provided by the fact that Henry Steinborn was considered the world's strongest man in his day (Rader, 1956a)—quite an accomplishment for a comparatively trim 5'8" 210-pound man (Willoughby, 1970).

Just after the turn of the century, Alan Calvert's Milo Barbell Company, the pioneer manufacturer of adjustable barbells, launched a bodybuilding publication, *Strength*, to help promote its products (Willoughby, 1970). In the 1930s, following a change in ownership and several in management, the young Mark H. Berry became the Milo editor (Smith, 1988a). Mark Berry's contributions to the Iron Game included serving as the coach of the American weightlifting team in both the 1932 and the 1936 Olympics (Grimek, 1988), but undoubtedly his most widespread and enduring contribution involved promoting heavy squats.

Championing heavy squats naturally resulted from all the publicity Mark Berry had been giving Henry Steinborn (Todd, 1988), and the fact that Mark was training at Siegmund Klein's gym, where Steinborn was always seen squatting, along with the gym's famous owner, the marvelously built lightweight lifting champion of that era, Sig Klein (Hise 1940b; Klein, 1964). Between Henry Steinborn and Sig Klein, Mark Berry had all the living proof he needed that heavy flat-footed squats were a remarkable exercise, and he set off to change the world by broadcasting this message. If Mark Berry needed any added encouragement to believe what he was urging others to do, he had only to look in the mirror, for his methods had added over fifty pounds of muscular bodyweight to his own small frame (Rader, 1941).

With the aid of squat racks, a number of Mark Berry's students in the 1930s used heavy, flat-footed squats. By working up to weights in the 300- to 500-pound range, they started to gain muscular bodyweight at previously unheard of rates (Paschall, 1954b). The gains in this period that resulted from these methods were so conspicuous that Mark Berry was said to have ushered in a "new era" as a result of his emphasis upon intensive training of the body's largest muscle groups (Wright, 1934, p. 33). The Milo publications were filled with dramatic success stories based on these methods (e.g., Berry, 1933d, 1934; cf. Rader, ca. 1938, 1941).

Foremost among the Berry-inspired trainees from this period was the man whom authorities generally credit with most dramatically demonstrating—if not defining—the precise methods Mark Berry promoted most heartily, the one and only Joseph Curtis Hise (Smith, 1988a). Spurred on by Mark Berry's writings (Berry, 1931, 1933a), J. C. Hise really got the ball rolling with his original self-directed bulk building experiment, which he described to Berry (Berry, 1932a). Hise continued to refine his methods until he had transformed himself into the first of the self-created 300-pound lifting "monsters" (Paschall, 1954b, p. 16).

Without pushing them to this extreme level, we are going to apply the basic principles developed by J. C. Hise, the principles that have been helping the average man get big and strong for over fifty years (Howell, 1988b). Because J. C. Hise—more than any other single man—inspired and promoted "the great deep knee bend craze" (Rader, ca. 1938, p. 10), it is well worth our time to become a little better acquainted with the man described as a "truly unsung genius of our sport" (Smith, 1988b, p. 2) and "truly a great man" (Jackson, 1988).

Joseph Curtis Hise was a colorful character whose legacy includes developing many of the exercise programs and dietary regimens that are still the most effective ways of getting big and strong. Although years of barbell training had already left the 5'8"* J. C. Hise weighing about 180 pounds, he was dissatisfied with his development and tried heavy, high-rep squats with forced breathing: As a result he gained twenty-nine pounds in a month—progress so remarkable that no one believed him (Rader, 1956). Refer-

---

*J. C. Hise's height has been reported as everywhere from 5'8" (Rader, 1956) to 5'10-1/2" (Drummond, 1934a). Hise had a theory that a strongman's height varied with his bodyweight (Hise, 1940a). The range in heights reported above is consistent with this relationship, as Hise weighed 180 pounds when reportedly 5'8" tall and he weighed 247 pounds when reportedly 5'10-1/2" tall!

ring to his initial progress, Hise would later note, "This was news with a bang" and the honorable Mark Berry withheld publishing Hise's description of his progress until local references verified his claims (Hise, 1940b, p. 14).

By his own example, Joseph Curtis Hise documented the supremely effective nature of the formula: heavy, breathing squats + wholesome food + milk + rest = incredible growth in muscular size and strength. And since Hise trained outdoors, using a squat rack made from tree limbs braced against the wall of a shed (Teegarden, 1988a), he also proved that the simplest equipment, properly employed, in even the crudest settings, can produce dramatic results. Hise pointed out to all who would follow his program that it would "make them junk all their clothes" (Berry, 1932b, p. 17).

"Brother Hise" (as Mark Berry referred to him) went on to develop power- and bulk-building programs based on exercises such as heavy, breathing squats; extremely heavy, breathing shrugs (see Howell, 1967, 1986); and heavy, stiff-legged deadlifts performed on a "hopper" (see Eells, 1940a and Rader, 1956); and in this capacity his importance "would be hard to over-emphasize" (Roark, 1988, p. 1). Underlining Hise's contributions, the Iron Game historian and authority Charles A. Smith has said that more than any other man, J. C. Hise is "entitled to be named 'Father of American Weight Training' " (Smith, 1988a, p. 2).

J. C. Hise's appetite for moving heavy iron was rivaled by his appetite for food and he was known to be quite an eater. The following account—from a report on the 1934 Senior National Weightlifting Championships—gives us an idea of what Hise could eat, his ability as a lifter, and why he is regarded as an interesting character:

Hise started to train for the contest on May 4th, which allowed him two weeks before he set out on Sunday the 20th to make the trip as best he could; he rode blind baggage into Pittsburgh where he was picked up by railroad detectives and lodged in jail for a day and night; from that point he made his way by freight to Philadelphia and managed to get a couple of days rest before striking out for the big town [Brooklyn, New York]. You should have seen that "man mountain" eat when he landed at Philly; not having eaten regularly for a few days he sat down to the table at something after midnight and ate steadily for over two hours, consuming a half gallon of coffee, much water, and unaccounted for stacks of solid grub . . . (Drummond, 1934b, p. 42)

Incidentally, J. C. Hise finished third in the contest and the great John C. Grimek failed to total, even though he was described as, "certainly the strongest man in the competition" (Drummond, 1934b, p. 43).

Mixing heavy breathing squats with serious eating eventually brought J. C. Hise to just over 300 pounds, although somewhere around 265 was considered his most impressive bodyweight (Howell, 1988a). So he got big, but did he also get strong? Yes. Some authorities might add qualifiers to British lifting expert W. A. Pullum's claim that the deadlift is "the fundamental test of a man's bodily strength" (Willoughby, 1970, p. 51), but it's probably as good a single measure as any, and back in 1935, J. C. Hise was deadlifting 700 pounds (Hise, 1941). This performance would have still been excellent thirty years later, in the first ("official") Senior National Powerlifting Championships. Based on the results J. C. Hise was producing, heavy, breathing squats were becoming a well documented results-producer (Howell, 1978), and the basic exercise attracted the interest of other innovators.

The next major development in the squat's evolution was based on Roger Eells's research, also begun in the 1930s, which stressed the importance of breathing technique, not the weight used, when squatting (Paschall, 1954b). In fact Eells's pupils—often using far less than bodyweight on the bar, with copious forced breathing in between each rep—used the "breathing squat" to mirror the bodyweight gains, at least initially, of the heavier squat programs, even if the strength gains were absent (Rader, 1956b, p. 20).* Explanations of why these light breathing squats were effective centered around two points: They isolated the crucial growth variable in the exercise equation—deep breathing—and they conserved energy for growth by not spending leg strength (Eells, 1940a). As with Mark Berry before him, Roger Eells explained that the best way to get a bigger upper body is to gain weight and "the way to gain weight is to specialize on your chest . . . and the way to specialize on your chest is to specialize on your legs . . . to specialize on your leg exercise you have no other choice than to specialize on BREATHING SQUATS!" (Eells, 1940b, p. 5). By now, a basic process was firmly established: breathe, squat, grow.

Between the examples set by Milo Steinborn and J. C. Hise, the squat was well on its way to becoming recognized as the master exercise, and even as Mark Berry and Roger Eells left the Iron Game, new proponents of the squat emerged. Two in particular are worth mentioning: Peary Rader and John McCallum.

Peary Rader, founder of *Iron Man* magazine and its editor and publisher for fifty years, "after twelve years of fruitless exercise on all other systems," gained ten pounds in his first month of squatting and nearly a hundred over

---

*Gains in strength following bodyweight breathing squats can sometimes be found. For example, Hise once managed to persuade his well-known trio of young Sacramento pupils (Lewis Parker, Bob Munfrey, and John Hechtman) to try these "peewee" squats, even though they were loath to squat with anything less than maximum weights. Not only did their chests expand, but their maximum squats increased as well (Hise, 1940b).

the next year or so (Rader, 1964, p. 24). Like so many others Peary's success resulted from reading about Hise's program, corresponding with him, and then following his advice (Rader, ca. 1938). In two years, using the squat program, Peary went from being a nearly six-foot 128-pound self-described "thin, weak being [who] didn't have the strength to hold a regular job for more than a month or so" to a lifting champion, a transformation Peary noted was not an isolated case (Rader, 1956b, p. 18). Combining the best elements of the prevailing systems, Peary advocated the following guidelines as the best basic squatting formula: twenty repetitions with all the weight one could handle, with three deep breaths in between each rep (Rader, 1964).

For a while Peary was alone in championing the squat. The other major publisher in the field, Bob Hoffman, condemned the exercise as harmful (Rader, 1955a). Hoffman later reversed his position and, through his magazines, provided a forum for spreading the benefits of squats to still more people.

John McCallum, like Peary Rader, began his squatting career as an inconspicuously muscled 140-pound six-footer, and he added over one hundred pounds of muscle to "the worst bone structure imaginable" in less than three years (McCallum, 1963, p. 48). In keeping with the tradition of one squat success story inspiring the next, it should be noted that John McCallum started squatting after reading old issues of *Iron Man*, wherein twenty-rep squats were being pushed as "great growth stimulators." As a result "John learned to squat, squat, squat" (Rader, 1967, p. 14). This progress made John a believer, and beginning in the mid-1960s he wrote the "Keys to Progress" series for the now-defunct magazine *Strength & Health*, once published by Bob Hoffman's York Barbell Company.

John's immensely popular and highly acclaimed series combined an unusual gift for writing with an intimate knowledge of the Iron Game. It now appears destined to become a classic, and anyone who reads even a few of his articles would be hard-pressed not to appreciate the simple truth that heavy squats work absolute wonders. For those of us who grew up reading about how John transformed his daughter's boyfriend, Marvin, from a pencil-neck into a muscleman, and followed John's wide-ranging training lectures to his ever-available buddy Ollie, entertainment was always at hand, and we became thoroughly impressed with the value of heavy—really heavy—squat programs. Remember what Mark Berry and Roger Eells said about squats? Listen to John McCallum:

> Your upper body bulk is determined by the size of your chest, and the size of your chest is determined by the size of your rib box . . . The surest, fastest way to enlarge your rib box is by combining deep breathing with heavy leg work . . . Heavy leg work and deep breathing will make your physique dreams come true. (McCallum, 1963, p. 24)

This should now be a familiar refrain.

Paul Anderson, possibly the strongest man in history and certainly the world's strongest man* in his day, was the last American super-heavyweight to win an Olympic gold medal in weightlifting (at Melbourne in 1956) and the last strongman to be a household name in the United States. Lest you think Paul's general prominence is being exaggerated, consider that he was selected by the U.S. State Department for a worldwide goodwill tour (Rader, 1956c)

---

*Titles such as "The World's Strongest Man" have been so abused that we are somewhat reluctant to even raise the subject. Nonetheless, if *any modern claimant* ever deserved such recognition, in our opinion—without question—it is Paul Anderson. This is hardly an isolated opinion. When asked whether he had any doubt *whatsoever* about whether Paul Anderson in his prime was the strongest man in the world, Peary Rader replied, "Absolutely none" (Rader, 1988). This shouldn't be surprising, since Peary often called Paul the "strongest man who ever lived" (Rader, 1969, p. 12).

and was featured across the media, from major national magazines to television news to the popular newsreels of the day (Paschall, 1956). Even a quick review will demonstrate what a prominent role the squat played in Paul's dramatic lifting successes.

Paul began weight-training as a 5'9" 190-pound teenage football player looking for a means to improve his performance. Within a short time, by training "almost exclusively" on the squat and drinking "many quarts" of milk a day, Paul soon weighed 275 pounds and was squatting close to 600 pounds (Rader, 1961, p. 20, 21). Shortly thereafter Paul began rewriting the weightlifting record books: With less than two years' training, Paul was approaching world records in the Olympic lifts, challenging Doug Hepburn as a candidate to be called the strongest man in history, and squatting absolutely phenomenal weights. The mere sight of Paul Anderson was enough to impress, as indicated in this report from the 1955 U.S. Senior national Weightlifting Championship:

> In this class we had the fabulous Paul Anderson from Toccoa, Georgia, and we do mean fabulous! You should hear the exclamations of amazement from the audience when he first walks out on the [lifting] platform. He is so huge [5'9" tall and 341 pounds] you can hardly believe it and yet he does not appear fat except a little around the waist. His legs, back, arms, and chest are all very hard. (Rader, 1955b, p. 28)

To better understand the significance of Paul's progress, let's take a closer look.

The year was 1952, and nineteen-year-old Paul Anderson, who had "used little else but the squat in his early training days" (Rader, 1954, p. 11), burst on the lifting scene: The official world record in the squat was 600 pounds (Lawson, 1956) and suddenly a teenager with less than one year's training was closing in on the mark. In mid-1953 Paul squatted 763 pounds, compared to Doug Hepburn's best of 665 pounds (Paschall, 1954a). By November 1953 Paul squatted 820 pounds (Glossbrenner, 1987). This was the era in which many authorities were calling Doug Hepburn the strongest man who ever lived and the young Paul Anderson, in a tremendous display of fundamental power, was far out-lifting him in the squat. By the mid-1950s Paul was squatting 900 pounds for repetitions. His equipment, rather than his strength, seemed to be the limiting factor (Lawson, 1956). As part of his stage show in the late 1950s Paul squatted with a phenomenal 1,160 pounds several times a night—forget the technological and pharmacological accoutrements of today's powerlifter, Paul didn't even have to warm up (Glossbrenner, 1987).*

Although he lagged behind Paul Anderson in terms of basic leg and back strength, Doug Hepburn went on to squat a remarkable 760 pounds in this same era (Willoughby, 1970). Interestingly, although Doug should certainly be mentioned in any conversation about the strongest men of all time, the fact that his feats of upper body strength were even more prodigious than those of his legs and back did not diminish his respect for the squat:

> Of all the exercises used to develop body power one stands alone. I am referring to the Deep Knee Bend or Squat. No other single exercise can give the trainee greater overall strength in return for the time and effort involved. (Hepburn, 1961, p. 29)

Strong words from a very strong man.

---

*Paul Anderson's feats under the squat bar transcend any analysis at the level of mere athletic performance, no matter how many superlatives are used. They dramatically demonstrate the formidable psychological process of true leadership (Strossen, 1988a,b).

Don't let all this talk about world-class power dissuade you from squatting if you are a bodybuilder. As long-time *Iron Man* author Bruce Page noted, "Of the hundreds of bodybuilding exercises being utilized today by weight training enthusiasts the world over, squats have by far the most bodybuilding potential of them all" (Page, 1960, p. 34). And remember, this includes building up your arms, shoulders, and chest.

What if you are focusing on improved strength, fitness, and development without necessarily putting a Mr. Universe title or a trip to the Olympics in your plans? What if you just want to gain a little functional, good-looking bodyweight? What can the squat do for you if you just want to get a little bigger? Listen to what the creator of the legendary, now-rare, Bosco training courses said: "Experienced weight trainers call the well-known deep-knee-bend THE GROWING EXERCISE" (Paschall, 1954b, p. 14). Squatting on this program is like putting your muscles in a greenhouse.

Finally, just in case you think that some ultramodern exercise has displaced the squat, listen to what the author of nearly all the best-selling contemporary books on bodybuilding has to say: "Virtually all the top bodybuilding champions have used heavy, high-rep squats in their training to give their body overall size" (Kennedy, 1983, p. 68) and, "Yes, the king of exercises, the squat, will help your overall gains along more than any other movement" (Kennedy, 1983, p. 113).

So there you have it—regardless of your specific training objectives, there is one absolutely peerless exercise for getting big and strong: the squat.

3 Your Program

Squats work whether you are a hard gainer or an easy gainer, whether you are primarily interested in adding muscular bodyweight or increasing your basic strength. If you are just starting to work out with weights, we recommend a well-rounded routine comprising the so-called basic exercises. If this proves ineffective, or you already know that you have to fight for every pound of muscular gains, we'll also outline a program that's about as certain to produce results as anything you'll ever find on earth.

The Basic Exercises

All the basic exercises are compound movements; that is, they work the muscles in groups, even if they focus on one particular area. Another way of looking at basic exercises is to note that they involve multiple joints (Leistner, 1988). For example, the bent over rowing exercise is generally thought of as primarily an upper back exercise, which it is. But bent-over rowing works more than the lattisimus dorsi ("lats"). It simultaneously gives the biceps muscles of the upper arm and all the flexor-related forearm muscles a good workout. And, while you are bent over at the hips, your wrists, elbows, and shoulders are in motion. So in fact, when you do bent-over rows, you are working everything along the path from one set of fingertips to the other!

This idea of working the muscles in groups is directly opposite the approach taken by many of the machines so

popular in contemporary gyms: Most machines are specifically designed to isolate a particular muscle and only involve moving one joint at a time. In this approach, for
example, the lats, the biceps, and the forearms would be
worked independently of each other.

Why would you ever want to work the muscles in
groups when you could isolate each one? Ignoring the fact
that your time is precious and you might not want to spend
three hours in the gym hitting each muscle group in turn,
and the fact that it's a rare movement in everyday life that
truly isolates a muscle group, there's another very compel-
ling reason to stick to the basic exercises: They increase
strength and size far more effectively than the isolation exercises (McCallum, 1967b). In fact one compound exercise
will produce far more bulk and power than an entire series
of isolation exercises. This was the radically new approach
to training pioneered by Mark H. Berry and Joseph C. Hise
(Wright, 1934).

The kicker is that the compound movements are also
more absorbing and seem naturally to focus your attention
on your training. As Dave Draper puts it:

> Wherever possible and without cheating, I prefer to in-
> volve the entire body in every movement. Thrust with
> form. Isolation has its place in training, but I find it
> boring, stiff and unexpressive. (Draper, 1988, p. 45)

Let's walk through the major muscle groups and review the
basic exercises for each.

Chest

The bench press is so popular today that it's hard to
imagine anyone who pumps iron not doing the movement,
but this is a recent trend. In the first half of the twentieth
century the leading bodybuilders generally weren't interested in heavy pectoral (chest muscle) development, and

now-standard bench pressing benches weren't common until well into the 1950s. And since the power lifts weren't yet official (and the press was still among the Olympic lifts), lifters didn't have a particularly good reason to practice the movement either.

Today when you talk about building up your chest, the conversation begins and often ends with bench presses. In addition to working the "pecs" (pectoral muscles), benches will give your triceps (back of the arms) and anterior deltoids (frontal shoulder muscles) a good workout. Benching with hand spacing a little wider than your shoulder width is recommended (the wider you go, the more relative stress you put on your pecs and anterior delts; the narrower you go, the more relative stress you put on your triceps). Stick to a flat bench initially, as opposed to an incline or decline bench. And, although it's okay to use a slight bounce off your chest, don't let the exercise degenerate into a two-arm bounce-arch-and-belly-toss. If you need to reinforce your motivation to bench press, remember that Doug Hepburn benched a whopping 580 pounds in 1954, and the effort wasn't lost on his upper body size or strength (Willoughby, 1970). In fact the current widespread popularity of the bench press has been attributed to the results it produced for Doug Hepburn and Marvin Eder (Todd, 1978). If you haven't heard of Marvin Eder before, keep reading.

A word of caution is in order here: Absolutely never do heavy bench presses without having spotters, a power rack, or safety stands to help you get out from under the bar if you can't complete the press. For all it's wondrous capabilities, the bench press can cause you a lot of discomfort and possibly even cost you your life if you ignore this simple advice. So play it smart and safe by making sure that you have a way to catch the bar in case you fail on a bench press. (See the section on Spotters that follows.)

An excellent alternative to the bench press is the parallel bar dip, working up to the point where you are tying heavy weights around your waist. It's been said by one who knows what he's talking about that dips will do almost as much for your upper body as squats will for your whole body (McCallum, 1967a). If you still need convincing, dig up pictures and lifting records of Marvin Eder.

There are very few bodybuilding or lifting stars from the 1950s who would still look good by today's standards. If you want to talk about the men whose accomplishments would still look good on both the posing dais *and* the lifting platform, the conversation might start and stop with Marvin Eder. And it just might not be coincidental that Marvin, at 197 pounds bodyweight, did a dip with 435 pounds in 1953—a staggering feat of upper body power (Willoughby, 1970). The same year, at the same bodyweight, Marvin did a 510-pound bench press (Willoughby, 1970). Remember, this is a man who looked like a bodybuilder.

So stick with bench presses or dips and for the time being, forget about all the flye-type exercises for the chest—whether done with cables, dumbbells, or machines, they just won't pack on the mass like benches or dips.

Shoulders

Overhead pressing is the name of the game here, but you have a few choices in terms of how you get the job done. Military presses, standing or seated; dumbbell presses, standing or seated, alternating sides or together; and presses behind the neck, standing or seated, are the main options. Since they all are effective, pick the one you can work on the hardest and switch to another when you start to go stale on the first. A couple of words on these overhead presses will help you make the most progress.

Back in the old days, a military press was a highly structured lift: Heels together, the press was done in harmony with the judge's slowly rising finger, and the back was so plumb straight that you had to press the barbell in a semicircle to get it around your chin! Compare that style to what was prevalent in the last days of the Olympic press* and you'll see why cannonball "delts" (deltoid muscles) weren't uncommon among the old-timers.

You don't have to be a fanatic about it, but if you keep your presses pretty strict you will work your shoulders and triceps to the hilt. The seated variations are offered not as a way to make the exercise stricter, but as a way to take the strain off the lower back. Some people who can squat, deadlift, and clean with nary a twinge in the lower back find that the first hard rep of a standing overhead press leaves their backs twisted in pain for days.

Don't be afraid to use really big weights on these overhead pressing movements. People have been doing so with great success for years: In the mid-1960s, weighing 215 pounds, Mel Hennessey did an extremely strict standing press behind the neck with 300 pounds (Cleveland, 1966); and the really big boys like Chuck Ahrens, Paul Anderson, and Doug Hepburn were all capable of pressing close to 400 pounds behind the neck thirty years ago (Willoughby, 1970). When your shoulders start to look like theirs, people will think you're wearing a padded suit.

Lateral raises are to the shoulders what flyes are to the chest. So forget them for the moment and concentrate instead on the bench presses and dips.

Upper Back

For the upper back the two major choices are bent-over rows or chins, but each has plenty of options. Let's talk about bent-over rowing first.

---

*The Olympic press was finally eliminated from weightlifting competition in 1972 because impartial officiating had become impossible in the face of the continually deteriorating standards. In fact things had gotten so out of hand that many lifters were pressing close to what they were cleaning and jerking.

The basic movement is done with a barbell, the upper body bent over parallel to the floor, and usually with a shoulder-width grip. Try to keep your back arched throughout the exercise to reduce the strain on your lower back. Pull the barbell up to the waist area and lower it, under control, back down to arm's-length before starting the next rep. Avoid the temptation to let the barbell swing or to put a little lower back into the exercise—just use your arms as hooks and your upper back muscles as the driver. To discover the pattern that feels best for you, experiment with different width grips and where you touch the barbell to your upper body. For example, some people can work their lats best by using a close grip (hands about six or eight inches apart) and pulling the bar to just above their hip bones. Others prefer a fairly wide grip and pull the bar to the bottom of the rib cage. For added variation try dumbbells, one at a time or together. If regular bent over rows with a barbell put too much strain on your lower back use a dumbbell, with your other hand braced against a bench for support.

Chins for the upper back are best done with the palms facing out and your hands spaced at a bit more than shoulder width. Pull up to your chest or the back of your neck, lower yourself fully, under control, and pull up again. Keep going, without swinging, until you can't do any more. Plan to start tying weights around your waist pretty soon, so get up to your full complement of sets and reps as quickly as possible—not by cheating on your style, but by just pulling with everything you've got on those last couple of reps. If you need a role model, think about Marvin Eder knocking off half a dozen reps with 125 pounds tied to his 197-pound body thirty-five years ago (Willoughby, 1970).

Although they all tend to work the upper back in compound movements, leave cable rows, T-bar rows, lat machines pulldowns and all the rest for later.

Arms

Most people like to load up on arm exercises. When they think about building big arm muscles, they usually picture the biceps, even though the triceps account for more arm bulk. We're going to take a different tack and greatly simplify things by emphasizing how arm training is the natural result of working other body parts. Let's start with the triceps.

If you are doing a pressing movement or two, such as the bench press and the press behind the neck, there's no reason right now to do any of the isolated triceps movements: French presses, pressdowns, kickbacks, and so on. Just work on your presses until your arms quiver, and your triceps will grow. If you have any doubts about the effectiveness of this approach, here are two ways to emphasize your triceps in the context of basic movements: Do heavy weighted dips instead of bench presses, or do your bench presses with a narrow- to medium-width hand spacing, while keeping your elbows close to your sides. Either of these approaches will help you build your triceps to levels of size and strength you might never have dreamed possible.

Your rows or chins will really take care of your biceps and forearms, but most people are stuck on the biceps as *the* vanity muscle, so we'll concede to including the basic barbell curl. Some people prefer to stand perfectly upright and others prefer to lean slightly forward when curling. Either way, do your curls in strict form for best results. That is, don't swing back to start the movement and be sure to lower the barbell under control—using a straight bar or an

EZ curl bar, as you prefer. Pull hard and maybe you can join the elite ranks of those who have done strict curls with over two hundred pounds. Later on you can try alternate dumbbell curls, incline curls, concentration curls, reverse curls, Scott bench curls, hammer curls, Zottman curls, and all the rest.

Thighs

It probably won't come as a surprise to learn that the squat is the exercise of first choice for your thighs. Specifically, you're going to do heavy, high-rep, parallel squats. The qualifier "breathing" could easily have been added to the list, but once you start doing these squats with the type of weight recommended, you will find that the breathing comes naturally!

Heavy—what does that mean? Regardless of how strong you are, two straightforward guidelines will determine your squat weight. First, you really are going to take your normal ten-rep poundage and do twenty reps with it. Second, you really are going to add five or ten pounds to the bar each and every single workout. We could add that you will make all your reps each workout because you really want to, and that by following the plan, you will gain size and strength at an unbelievable rate. What you do is a matter of your determination, and your actions will dictate your results: "Squat 200 pounds and you'll get strong enough to squat with 200 pounds; use 500 and become a Hercules" (McCallum, 1963, p. 48). Remember that lots of men have gotten up to 300-pound squats on this program; we're not saying it's easy, but if they can do it, why can't you? But, you say, "They probably started off a lot stronger than I am." Horse feathers! Peary Rader began the squat program using 35 pounds for ten reps and worked up to well over 300 pounds for twenty reps (Rader, ca. 1937).

High-rep means twenty reps as the basic program, but don't worry, you only have to do one set. For variety, especially if you stick with this program for more than six weeks or so at a stretch, you can try alternating two sets of fifteen reps or three sets of ten reps with the basic approach. You also might like to try going the other direction and work on one set of thirty repetitions. Don't be afraid to experiment, in the tradition of J. C. Hise, who continually developed and tested new approaches to what he often called "man making." Initially, however, you should stay with the well-proven formula of one set of twenty repetitions.

The parallel business might sound confusing after all the references to the deep knee bend, but don't let that name throw you. Only squat down until the tops of your thighs are parallel* to the floor, because that's all it takes to work the muscles properly. When you go into a full squat you greatly increase the risk of injuring your lower back with improper form.

So what's proper form? Keeping your back flat is the basic principle.** It's also a good idea to avoid bouncing at the bottom, especially if you squat to rock bottom, although a hard drive back up is recommended. The objective here is to avoid unnecessary strain on your knees, but not to intentionally rise in slow motion: Use muscular rebound to ram the weight back up once you hit parallel, but don't collapse under the weight and sink to rock bottom, trying to get some bounce at the end of the line. If you keep

---

*If you have any questions about your precise squat depth, err on the side of just breaking the parallel plane, rather than coming up a couple of inches too high.

**Serious students of Iron Game history will immediately wonder about this advice, because J. C. Hise was such a staunch proponent of round-back squats (Hise, 1940c). Since round-back squats necessarily increase the stress on the lower back and because your unique physical structure will largely dictate your precise squatting style, *aim* for the flattest back position you can reasonably maintain.

your back flat, it's just about impossible to injure it doing a squat, so spend a few minutes smoothing out your technique. A mirror or a knowledgeable observer are great learning aids, but here are two basic guidelines that should put—and keep—you on the right track.

First, always keep your eyes fixed on an imaginary spot at about head-height. By looking up as you lower yourself into and rise out of the squat (this is called "leading with your head"), you will almost automatically keep your back flat. The second important point is to remember to keep your shoulders rising at least as fast as your hips as you recover from the bottom of the squat (competitive power lifters might try for maximum squat poundage by letting their hips initially rise well ahead of their shoulders, but that's not the game you are playing now). A little forward lean is fine, but think in terms of squatting up and down with your back fairly close to vertical. As you bend forward, you load up the stress on your lower back and by the time your hips are rising faster than your shoulders, a rounded back—and strained muscles—are within easy reach. If it's difficult for you to maintain the correct position while squatting flat-footed at first, try putting a board or a barbell plate under your heels—but be sure that whatever you use is secure, and try to squat flat-footed as soon as you become flexible enough to maintain your balance. For our purposes, the flat-footed squat is preferred because it puts a heavier load on the largest muscles.

Let's do a couple of reps together. First, to help save your toughness for the actual squats, wrap a towel or piece of dense foam rubber around the bar to pad your upper back and shoulders—but don't use too thick a pad, or the bar will tend to slip off your back! Second, dip under the bar and take one step backward—the distance and the direction of this journey are important because if you work on the squats as hard as you should, you won't be able to manage any more than one forward step to the racks to return the barbell. Third, plant your feet solidly, at about shoulder width and with your toes pointed out. Don't do anything artificial with your foot placement—the correct stance should come naturally. Fourth, carry the bar fairly low on your shoulders, to cut down the strain on your lower back, but be sure to find a rock-solid position. Now you're ready to squat.

Head up, eyes on the imaginary spot, and take three deep breaths. Deep. DEEPER. *STILL DEEPER.* Open your mouth wide to suck in all the air you possibly can. Hold the last breath and squat to parallel—when you hit parallel, drive up and blast out the air at the same time. Holding your breath is tempting, as you put out a maximum effort, but it's also the ticket to passing out. Here's what you do: Think of your mouth as the nozzle of a garden hose and, as you rebound from parallel, begin to exhale in a narrow, high-pressure stream. As you get past the sticking point, open your mouth wide (just like the nozzle on a hose) and empty out your lungs as quickly as you can. Standing up again, adjust your eyes and the bar if you need to, take three deep breaths, squat, drive up, and exhale. That's the pattern. Remember that three lung-bursting breaths is the minimum between each rep, and once you get above the tenth rep you might be taking half a dozen or more breaths.*

To gain the last bit of chest expansion from these squats, here's a tip provided by no less an authority than J. C. Hise's good friend James E. Douglass: After you have taken your last full breath before dropping down into your

---

*This business about how many breaths to take in between each repetition of the 20-rep squats can get confusing. For example, the general recommendation of at least three breaths for each rep might sound confusing when you might actually prefer to knock off the first few reps with only one breath on each rep, but might be taking ten breaths between each of the last five reps. The important point is that you should be breathing like a steam engine for at least half the repetitions and the best way to ensure this is to *average* at least three breaths per rep for the entire set.

squat, take one last gulp on top of your already full lungs (Douglass, 1988b). You won't believe the difference this last mouthful of air can make on your gains.

Another hint for maximizing your results from these squats will sound like absolute heresy to contemporary powerlifters: Don't wear a lifting belt while doing these squats! A shocking idea, clearly, but my personal experience has demonstrated that wearing a lifting belt significantly inhibits your breathing and doesn't really make a noticeable difference in terms of avoiding back fatigue on these squats. Although this approach seems so unorthodox today, a poll of some of the most experienced experts on the subject discovered that most of the men who pioneered this program *never* used lifting belts while squatting (Douglass, 1988b; Rader, 1988). So, if your mind can handle it, your body will likely benefit if you do these squats without wearing a lifting belt.

The squat is the key to this whole program. So, at the risk of repetition, let's listen to how the grand master, John McCallum, summarizes its role and execution:

[Oddy Hansen, a tall and skinny firefighter, has sought the help of an unusually knowledgeable gym owner: Oddy wants to get big and strong. The gym owner has explained that heavy breathing squats are the "ultimate exercise for building bulk and power," underlined the need to do them right and has demonstrated proper squatting technique (McCallum, 1972, p. 63). Here the gym owner is summarizing the key element in Oddy's program.]

"You're gonna do one set of twenty reps," he said. "And it's gotta be the hardest work you've ever done. You gotta be absolutely annihilated when you finish. If you can even think of a second set, then you're loafing. All the muscle you'll ever build depends on how hard you work on this one set of squats."

"How much weight should I use?" Oddy asked.

"You pick a weight you can do ten reps with," the gym owner said, "and then you do twenty reps with it."

Oddy stared at him. "You're putting me on."

"No way," the gym owner said. "Each rep from ten on should feel like the end. But you use your mind. You grit your teeth and blank out everything else and you take the reps one by one, until you've done all twenty."

"Then," the gym owner said, "when you finish, do one set of light pullovers to stretch your rib cage. Do twenty reps with about twenty pounds." (McCallum, 1972, p.76)

Squat hard and get big.

Even though the necessity of working hard has been raised a number of times, you might still be doubting it. Don't. "Right here I'll say that if you are afraid of work please don't try the squat program. Be satisfied with your present skinny condition and try and get as much fun from life as your condition allows" (Rader, circa 1938, p. 26).

And, just in case you think you can fool the system and get results without putting forth a tremendous effort, be forewarned: "You might as well not do them at all if you don't intend to put all you've got into them" (Rader, ca. 1939b, p. 15). If you need an image of what really hard work entails, think of the Herculean World War II-era weightlifter, Louis Abele, who said his efforts "caused such violent breathing that my teeth ached" (Teegarden, 1948, p. 14). That's the spirit!

As marvelous as it is, the squat has not been without its critics. Chief among their points is the reputed risk to one's knees. It certainly seems possible that improper use of squats could lead to knee injuries, but I have never heard of properly performed squats resulting in a single case of knee injury. In fact, consistent with the most current research (Herrick, Stone and Herrick, 1987), I have often seen squats used to help rehabilitate injured knees and to prevent knee injuries. But check first with your physician if you have any doubts. It should also be pointed out that the research underlying criticism of the squat as detrimental to the knees contained some extremely serious design flaws—flaws that compromise its conclusions.*

Spotters. Without exaggeration, getting stuck under a heavy squat is a most unpleasant and potentially disastrous experience. Fortunately it's also very easy to avoid. If at all possible only squat with spotters: One person at each end of the bar is preferred, but simply having one person standing behind you is infinitely better than nothing. The spotters are there to help you up, should you be unable to rise with the barbell. And they will greatly boost your confidence—leading to heavier weights.

If you can't use spotters squat in a power rack, or use safety stands—anything that will allow you to walk away from the loaded barbell if you can't rise from the bottom of a squat. These safety devices need not be fancy: saw horses, strong wooden boxes, and chains hung from overhead beams have all been used to ensure safe squatting. Above all, test your safety device before you begin to rely upon it. NEVER, EVER, DO HEAVY SQUATS WITHOUT OBSERVING THESE PRECAUTIONS.

Hate Squats?. Don't worry if you find squats unpleasant—you're normal, and that's to be expected. Paul Anderson, the greatest squatter of all time, said that because they are "the most torturous of all weight training movements"

---

*For a discussion of this controversy and a review of the methodology employed by the squat's chief critic, see Todd, 1984.

CHAPTER 3 / YOUR PROGRAM 53

he used to "dread" squats (Anderson, 1964, p. 22). Actually, almost nobody enjoys squats at first because, after all, some of their qualities are less than endearing: the Herculean amount of labor involved, the pressure of the bar across your shoulders, the fear of getting flattened by the barbell, and so forth. Now that we've established that it's reasonable to initially dislike squats, what's next?

A key here is the point about disliking squats *initially*, because if you stick with them for a little while, the results they produce will hopefully convert you to, first, a reluctant-but-willing squatter and then an outright-zealous squatter. Help speed up this transition by following all the instructions from padding the bar to using spotters, right down to the last words of advice on diet and attitude. You will be amazed at how quickly the results produced by following this program will make you a diehard squatter, so don't quit before you even start. This advice applies in spades to 20-rep squats:

> Twenty rousing reps, and blow out hard when you exhale. Some of you complain that you can't do 20 of these. If you can't, you are missing the BIG benefits. We personally never gained until we got the reps to twenty. (Paschall, 1952, p. 50)

The good news is that you only have to do one set, the results will absolutely astound you, and you'll probably never again encounter such hard work in anything else you do. And, above all, remember that these squats are a means to an end: "Most of us have no love for the DKB [deep knee bend]—what we want is the big chest, the wide shoulders, the great bodily power that it nourishes" (Hise, 1940c, p. 24). You don't have anything against getting a big chest or wide shoulders, do you?

Rib Cage

In their descriptions of why heavy, high-repetition squat programs work, everyone from Mark Berry to John McCallum has emphasized the primary role played by the rib cage in determining upper body muscle mass potential, and how the squats can expand it.

The furious breathing that is nearly unavoidable when doing a lot of squats with heavy weights, and which you will specifically cultivate, sets the stage for significant rib cage growth. To capitalize on this opportunity you should immediately follow your squats with a rib cage expansion exercise. These exercises are designed to maximize the growth potential following your heavy leg work—and since they involve light weight or none at all, they should be a welcome break from heaving big iron. The two basic choices—stiff-armed pullovers or Rader chest pulls—both rely on the same principle of stretching the rib cage.

To do stiff-armed pullovers, grab a light weight, say fifteen or twenty pounds, and lie on a bench. For weight, any of the following will do: a barbell, one dumbbell, a pair of dumbbells, or a barbell plate. Position yourself lengthwise or crosswise on the bench, whichever feels better.* Take a deep breath, raise the weight over your head, and allow a good stretch to develop as you lower the weight as far as possible. Exhale as you return the weight to the starting position. The reason for using a *light* weight in this movement is that you don't want your muscles to contract. That would defeat your purpose, and the only reason any weight is being used is to facilitate the stretching process. If you want to get the very most out of this exercise, at the ex-

---

*The phrase "whichever feels better" refers to the goal of stretching your rib cage and not a general sense of bodily comfort. The bitter truth is that the most effective exercises for stretching your rib cage are somewhat uncomfortable to perform. Because putting up with a little discomfort, in this case, pays big dividends in terms of advancing muscular growth, any related growing pains are welcomed by serious trainers (Hise, 1941).

pense of your immediate personal comfort, perform it in the specialized manner developed by Charles A. Ramsey:* Keep your hips on the floor, with your upper back supported on a low bench (Teegarden, 1942).

A less well-known exercise for the same purpose as stiff-armed pullovers is the Rader chest pull (Rader, 1951; Page, 1986). It takes a bit of learning, but can provide benefits far exceeding standard pullovers. To perform this exercise grab an immovable object about the height of your head, take a deep breath, and simultaneously pull down and inward. You can use a door jamb, an upright on a power rack, the top of a refrigerator, or just about anything else that is roughly the height of the top of your head and will allow you to pull down and toward yourself. As you pull you should feel your rib cage arch upward, although you might have to experiment with different grips and polish your technique for maximum benefits. You can do Rader chest pulls with slightly bent arms or straight arms and, as with pullovers, you should try to keep your abdominal muscles from contracting when performing the movement.

Properly done, these exercises will produce a definite pulling sensation in the sternum (proof that they are working), and you can bring your chest to the point of outright soreness and pain. So use a little prudence and expand your rib cage, but don't torture yourself.

Whichever rib cage exercise you choose, feel free to use it after other exercises besides the squat, as well as in between your regular workouts. Citing their benefits, Dave

*Charles A. Ramsey deserves more than a footnote. Among other things he was an Oxford-educated British gentleman who was personally trained by the great Eugen Sandow as a youth, went on to become a champion wrestler, opened bank branches around the world for what is now Citibank, lived in Harlem, and as a voluntary community service ran a neighborhood club from which he produced many outstanding lifters (Ramsey, 1940; Pride, 1954). For our immediate purposes, know that J. C. Hise called Charles A. Ramsey "doubtless the greatest individual trainer of the present age" (Hise, ca. 1938)

Draper mixes dumbbell pullovers "with nearly every-thing" (Draper, 1988, p. 38). Also, remember that a few minutes of stretching won't offset the negative effects of continuous poor posture. If you don't already have enough good reasons to stand and sit with your back straight, your shoulders back and your chest up, following this 20-rep squat program will soon give you so much self-pride that you won't be able to avoid good posture!

Lower Back

Even if you squat in a very strict style, with your upper body as vertical as possible, your lower back will get a good workout, so good that many trainees won't find it neces-sary to do any work specifically aimed at their lower backs. For those who want to give this area, along with the hips and thigh biceps (back of the thigh), some extra work, we recommend the stiff-legged deadlift.

Stiff-legged deadlifts were one of the primary leg exer-cises advocated around the turn of the century (Paschall, 1954b). Their potential for contributing to one's strength and muscular mass are only a notch down from the squat, but the exercise—with heavy weights—is not done too frequently anymore. At least three factors work against the deadlift's popularity:

1. After doing heavy squats, heavy deadlifts are usual-ly the last thing anyone wants to do (more squats notwithstanding).
2. Because of the large muscle groups involved and the heavy weights used, deadlifts are just plain a lot of work no matter when you do them.
3. With a lot of concern about the potentially delicate lower back, many trainers and trainees prefer to not work the area with anything quite so direct.

Your motivation will handle the first two concerns, but what of the third? Ironically many people have found that heavy, properly done stiff-legged deadlifts and a dose of common sense are the best prescription going for avoiding back problems.

Be very careful to maintain your form, so as not to turn your stiff-legged deadlifts into so-called "hospital reps," done with stiff legs, rounded back, and the head down (Benjamin, 1983, p. 36). Most people prefer to do these deadlifts while standing on a low platform, so the bar can be lowered all the way to the tops of their feet, but others prefer the opposite: Hise developed a wooden frame "hopper" to bounce the bar through the bottom portion of the movement (see Eells, 1940a, Rader, 1946).* You can put a slight bend in your legs to take the pressure off your knees, but once in position, keep them locked in position. Just as with the squat, keeping your head *up* will help you keep your back *flat*, which is a key for building your back rather than breaking it.

If you want to maintain an image of what the stiff-legged deadlift can do for you in terms of building power and muscle, think about John Grimek, who used to knock off reps with 400 to 500 pounds in ultra-strict style (Paschall, 1954b).

Calves

Most people would just as soon skip their calves when on a bulk and power routine, but if you want to throw in the basic toe raise, that's fine. You can reduce the monot-

---

*To picture how a hopper works, visualize propping up a wooden plank by putting a brick under each end. Do the same thing with another plank, parallel to the first, and adjust the width between the two planks so that you can rest your barbell on them (one end of the loaded barbell goes on one plank and the other end goes on the other plank). You're now ready to bounce the barbell off this makeshift hopper.

ony by varying whether your feet are turned in or out, but always go through the full range of motion—all the way up on your toes and all the way down, without bouncing.

Want to work your calves, but lack a sophisticated calf machine for toe raises? No problem. Nail a short piece of 4-by 4-inch lumber to a larger board (to keep it from flipping over), round the top edge and pad it if you want to get fancy, and you are all set. If even this sounds too complicated, stand on a step, a curb, or any other immobile object of suitable height. Work one leg at a time, holding onto something for balance with one hand and a dumbbell with the other when you need more resistance.

As usual, plan to work into heavy weights. All-time physique great Reg Park was doing twelve reps of two-legged toe raises with 800 pounds when Arnold Schwarzenegger first visited him twenty years ago (Schwarzenegger and Hall, 1979).

Abdominals

Having strong abdominals is more than merely an aesthetic concern, as they will help improve your posture, prevent ruptures and support your entire upper body. So give your stomach muscles a little work by throwing in a set or two of your favorite abdominal exercise: crunches, leg raises, bent-leg sit-ups, and so on. You don't have to spend hours slaving away on the incline board, but don't neglect this vital area.

General Points

Style

We recommend a fairly strict exercise style for the basic exercises. Don't fall into the trap of using a sloppy style as a way to artificially boost your workout poundages, thinking that you are getting your muscles to do more work. Since the basic exercises utilize multiple muscle groups, they naturally lend themselves to heavy weights even when you maintain a strict exercise style. Remember that the correct style is defined so as to work the target muscles; any deviation from this style simply transfers some of the work to another muscle group. Such cheating is usually disadvantageous. For example, if you do nothing but swing your upper body back and forth a lot when you do barbell curls, it can be argued that you have taken a good arm exercise and turned it into a poor back exercise. On the other hand there's nothing wrong with cranking out every last rep you can in good style and then doing one or two more with as little cheating as it takes to complete the movement.

Selection and Progression of Training Poundages

Start with moderate poundages, especially if you haven't been training hard on a regular basis, and gradually increase the weights you are using. "Moderate poundages" means weights that allow you to perform all your designated repetitions in immaculate style, and without busting a gut. You "gradually increase" the weight by adding five or ten pounds to the bar each time you can complete all your reps.

Except for the squat, you will probably hit a point where, after your latest increase in your training poundage, you can't make your full complement of repetitions. That's fine—just stick with the new weight until you can drill your required reps, and then increase the weight again. For example, you might be doing bench presses in sets of twelve repetitions and after knocking off your full twelve with 175 pounds you add ten pounds to the bar in your next workout, only to find that you run out of gas at the ninth rep. Stay with your new weight, 185 pounds, until you can do all twelve reps, before you make your next increase.

On the squats you should also start with a moderate poundage, but your progression will be very simple: Add five or ten pounds to the bar every single workout and make all twenty repetitions each time!

Stretching

Always start with a few minutes of stretching. Don't make the common mistake of thinking that you don't need to or that you have too little time to stretch. Stretching will not only leave you more flexible, but it will end up saving you workout time by allowing you to blast through your weight program faster, with muscles that are already primed for work. Stretching will also minimize your chances of getting injured, and injuries are the single most effective roadblock to your progress. If you think such a big, strong person as yourself doesn't need to fool around touching his toes, doing dislocates, hip and arm circles, and so on, just watch what the weightlifters who can clean and jerk over 500 pounds do before they get close to a loaded barbell.

Warming Up

After stretching, the next step in priming your muscles is to run through some warm-ups with fairly light weights. Don't think this is a waste of time. A proper warm-up will help you feel good in your workout, it will help you lift heavier weights, and it will help you avoid injuries. All those things spell progress. It could also be said that if you don't have time to warm up, you don't have time to train.

How much of a warm-up is necessary and what are some different ways you can run through this part of your training? Most people begin each exercise with a light set or two, increasing the weight as they warm up. If they are doing low-rep sets (for example, five or fewer reps per set), most people will do at least two warm-up sets, progressively heavier, for each exercise. If they are doing higher rep sets (say, at least ten reps per set), many people find that a general warm-up set or two, at the beginning of their program, is enough. Another commonly used approach involves using the general warm-up for everything except the really heavy poundage exercises (such as squats), where a specific warm-up set or two is performed.

For an effective general warm-up, try an exercise that involves all the major muscles and noticeably increases your pulse and your breathing: power cleans (with or without a press on each rep), dumbbell swings, and flip snatches are excellent choices. Try about a dozen reps with a moderate weight.

Use your head in terms of figuring out how much and what type of warm-up works best for you. When in doubt, err on the side of doing too many warm-up exercises rather than too few.

Equipment

As we claimed in the beginning of this book, and as demonstrated by the descriptions of the basic exercises, it really doesn't take a lot of fancy equipment to build a bigger, stronger body. You can follow this program at home just as well as in any commercial gym. In fact most of the slick computerized or cam-driven machines just won't do the trick as well as the basics of a barbell, a bench, and squat racks.

Pick your equipment based on its function, not its appearance. Strength is far and away the most important quality for good equipment. This should seem obvious, but when you see people doing heavy bench presses on something that's swaying mightily under the load, you have to wonder about just how prevalent common sense really is. Without going to the extremes of having a bench collapse on you in the middle of a set of bench presses, the one-time thrill of having a dumbbell come apart while overhead should convince even the thickest-headed trainee that rugged equipment is the right tool for the job.

All you really need to follow the *Super Squats* program is a good exercise bar with sound collars, a set of squat racks, a bench, a method for spotting, lots of weight, and the desire to lift it.

The bar might not be quite as simple as it sounds, although the crudest five-foot long, one-inch diameter hot-rolled steel bar will do for starters. A cold-rolled steel bar is a lot better because of its superior strength. Ideally, it should be six or seven feet long. If money is no object, you can rush out and buy the finest quality Olympic lifting bar and half a ton of bumper plates, but you can get the same quality workout with a bar and plates for a fraction of that cost.

Although you don't see them that frequently, the best value in the way of an exercise bar, if you're serious, is to buy an Olympic lifting bar, minus the revolving sleeves. This way you get a top quality bar—with all the life of a fine lifting bar—without the added cost of the revolving sleeves and Olympic-style plates. Check around for manufacturers who sell their finest bars with or without the revolving sleeves. This will cut the cost of your bar to less than half of what it would otherwise be and save you a comparable amount every time you buy barbell plates. A notch less desirable but still far superior to a basic sporting-goods-store bar would be a seven-foot long bar of steel specially processed for more brute strength. This bar won't have the zip of an Olympic lifting bar, but at least you won't have to worry about it bending with the mighty weights you will be using. Be sure that your bar is not over

1 1/16 inches in diameter, as most exercise plates are bored with 1 1/8-inch holes. There's nothing more aggravating than to have someone give you a pair of fifty-pound plates, only to find that they won't fit on your bar!

Barbell plates come in widely varying grades and prices and the two don't always go hand in hand. If you remember to buy your plates based on what they weigh, not what they look like, you can save a lot of money. Many illustrious people from the past used fly wheels, tractor wheels, and other crude items as a perfectly acceptable complement to their manufactured barbell plates. One nice thing about barbell plates is that you don't have to rush out and buy 1,200 pounds the first day—you can add them a couple of plates at a time. Unless you have a twelve-foot bar to hold the bulky and flimsy sand-filled vinyl plates, go for either solid metal plates or, if money is no object, top quality bumper plates.

Make sure your collars are secure—some, no matter how mighty they look, simply cannot be fastened securely without using a sledgehammer. This means that they are pretty useless as they will rarely be put in place tightly enough to do their job, which is to keep the plates on the bar, no matter which direction the bar is facing. Having secure collars is absolutely imperative for your dumbbells, too. Always test your collars before you lift the bells over your face for the first time. If you don't, keep the name of a good orthodontist handy.

Benches come in umpteen varieties, but a solid flat bench will get you by and one with bench-pressing uprights will be hot stuff for our purposes. If you want to get fancy you can pick out a bench with an adjustable incline and with adjustable uprights, or you can even get a bench with both of those features plus integrated spotting racks. All-welded heavy-gauge steel benches are preferred, but others can be satisfactory. In addition to taking a good look at its basic construction, the weight of a bench is a pretty fair way to estimate its overall strength. Especially if you are willing to stick with a basic flat bench, you can build something perfectly serviceable with hand tools and heavy lumber.

Squat racks are the other big item on the equipment list. They can be traditional freestanding uprights on heavy bases, a power rack, a step-style rack, and so on. Once again, strength is the chief requirement and the exact form is distinctly secondary in importance. Tremendous ingenuity has been used to muster up suitable squat racks. Remember how J. C. Hise used sawed-off tree limbs braced against a shed (Teegarden, 1988a)? Urban trainees have been just as creative—I know someone who trained in the kitchen of his San Francisco condominium and used two solid bar stools for a squat rack. Another urbanite developed a collapsible rack that he braced on his bedroom dresser when being used and later stored under his bed (Salvati, 1964).

Don't forget the advice on the need for spotters when doing squats and bench presses. Select your equipment accordingly.

Workout Schedules

Here are a couple of alternative workout schedules that will put you on the road to tremendous gains in size and strength, and provide the type of exercise conducive to better health. In each of these programs start with moderate poundages and increase them steadily.

The Basic Routine

The basic program is built around the heavy, 20-rep squats. This is an excellent program for anyone whose training history shows a good response to working out, or for the person who is just starting out. If you have always had to struggle for each pound of muscular bodyweight, skip this routine and use the Abbreviated Program presented below.

This basic routine might look pretty streamlined compared to all the super-duper programs being pushed by muscledom's flashiest marketers, but don't be fooled: This is very close to the maximum number of exercises one can reasonably use for fast gains and, in all likelihood, you can speed up your gains by cutting back on even this program. The basic routine should take less than an hour to complete.

Seated press behind the neck	3 × 10
Bench press	3 × 12
Bent over rowing	2 × 15
Standing curl	2 × 10
Parallel squat	1 × 20
Rader chest pull	1 × 20
Stiff-legged deadlift	1 × 15
Rader chest pull	1 × 20
Toe raises	3 × 20
Crunches	1 × 25

Remember to maintain your form on each exercise and feel free to substitute movements as described above. For example, you might prefer military presses to seated presses behind the neck or stiff-armed pullovers to Rader chest pulls, or you might wish to do straight bar curls for a while and then switch to an EZ curl bar.

The Abbreviated Program

If you have problems gaining weight on the basic program, try this:

Bench press	2 × 12
Parallel squat	1 × 20

Rader chest pull	1 × 20
Bent over rowing	2 × 15

This program has worked some absolute miracles on people whose bodies defied development on countless other exercise programs, and these three exercises—the bench press, squat, and bent-over rowing—are Peary Rader's precise recommendation for "great results, both in the legs and the upper body" (Rader, 1964, p. 25). Just remember to work absolutely as hard as you possibly can on these exercises: Fight for every last rep and try to add weight to the benches and rows every workout, exactly as in the squats.

Training Frequency

Most people work out three times a week on this program, on alternate days, such as Monday, Wednesday, and Friday. Quite a few people will find that they cannot recover properly from this level of training and therefore do better training twice per week, such as on Monday and Thursday. Still other people will find that, at least on the squats, they do best to train only every fifth or sixth day. Adjust your program to meet your needs and don't be afraid to develop an individual formula, such as training three times per week, but only including the squats on two of those days.

How can you distinguish between a bona fide case of incomplete recovery and imaginary aches and pains stemming from laziness or a close cousin? Light soreness should not keep you from training, as it will fade with your first warm-up set. "Incomplete recovery" means a deep-down muscle ache, something that tells you the muscle is about to be traumatized if you force another training session before you have recuperated. Another indicator is your pulse. Start taking your pulse in the morning, shortly after you rise. If your pulse is elevated, chances are good that you still haven't recovered from your last workout. In this case rest, rather than more training, is called for.

Make no mistake about it: You can always force yourself through one more training session before you have recovered from the last one, but your reward will be a *loss* of both muscle size and strength. Err on the side of overdoing the rest, but remember, too, that if you don't ever train, you also won't gain.

The question of properly balancing training and recovery might sound more complicated than it actually is. Start off training three times a week. If your legs are still painfully sore when the time for your next workout rolls around, give yourself an extra day off in between training sessions. If they are still sore, plug in another rest day and so forth. Conversely, if you have been training twice a week, recovering fine, and are interested in trying a third training session per week, go ahead.

Alternating Programs

It's impossible to keep gaining forever, but the key to making steady progress is to avoid long-term staleness. One of the best ways to do this is by alternating your routines before you get severely overtrained. In fact alternating your routines can sometimes prove to be as refreshing as a complete break from training.

The key to effective program planning is to alternate programs that complement each other but are sufficiently different to give your mind and body an invigorating sense of novelty. For example, the heavy 20-rep squat program builds basic bulk and power, so it wouldn't be effective to alternate this program with a crash diet, aerobics-oriented program. It would make sense, however, to alternate this program with a power program based on lower reps, higher sets, and possibly more exercises.

The low-rep power program is a natural for these purposes because it shares the major goals of your 20-rep squat program, but takes a very different form of attack. Here's a sample of a program you might want to alternate with your 20-rep squat program:

Power cleans	5 × 5
Alternate dumbbell press	5 × 5
Incline bench press	5 × 5
Upright rows	5 × 5
Alternate dumbbell curls	5 × 5
Parallel squats (with a set of light pullovers following each set of squats)	5 × 5
Leg raises	2 × 25

As with your 20-rep squat program, use this routine as an example of how to structure your workouts, but substitute specific exercises as you wish. If you alternate, say, six weeks on this type of program with six weeks on the 20-rep squat program, you will stay fresh and can sustain tremendous progress in terms of building muscle mass and strength.

Another way to maintain your growth, but also give yourself a break from the specific demands of the 20-rep squat program, is to mix in some cycles built along the same lines as your basic routine, but which work the squats in either three sets of ten to twelve repetitions, or in two sets of fifteen repetitions. Either of these can prove to be a refreshing change from your basic approach and will keep you growing like a weed. On the 3 × 10 to 12 approach, use the same weight for all three sets, but on the 2 × 15 program, use your maximum for the first set and then drop down a full hundred pounds for your second.

And you thought only East Germans and Russians could get big and strong!

4 The Other Factors: Diet, Rest, and Attitude

So far *Super Squats* has concentrated on the exercise portion of the growth equation. But, as implied by our discussion of work-out frequency, exercise alone will not build a bigger and stronger body. The other three factors are diet, rest, and attitude.

Diet

Both mainstream thinking about nutrition and the leading-edge approach taken by iron athletes have changed enormously since the days when J. C. Hise devotees first chased their heavy, high-repetition squats with gallons of milk. Today the general public is probably more aware than ever before about how diet influences well-being, and it's a rare person who isn't careful about some aspect of his diet, whether he's watching his intake of salt, sugar, calories, saturated fat, preservatives, or what have you. The funny thing here is that what worked for the Hise clan—eating lots of protein-rich food—is still a sure-fire way to grow some very serious muscle.

As bodybuilders and lifters began to seriously pursue the development of muscular bulk, they naturally evolved toward a preference for high-protein, high-calorie diets. Naturally, that is, because muscle is built from protein, and calories are the basic unit of energy. From these two facts it was only a short step to the inference that if you wanted to build more muscle, you should increase your body's supply of protein and calories. Thus the high-protein, high-calorie pattern defined the standard for gaining weight and, in addition, had the following benefits attributed to it: increased physical energy, strength, and measurements, along with the retention of a high degree of muscular definition (Stephens, 1963).

Milk, without question, was and still is the food of first choice for the traditional approach to bulking up: It is high in protein, rich in other nutrients, easy to consume in large quantities, and—the proof of the pudding—everyone on these heavy squat programs who drank enough of it gained weight. Yes, *everyone* we've ever heard of.

How much milk is enough? The general advice is to drink at least two quarts a day, which might sound like a lot if you're new to this routine. Actually you should treat this as a bare minimum if you are serious about getting bigger, and a gallon a day should be your goal. Don't be discouraged by this amount—it's pretty manageable if you keep drinking a glass here and there throughout the day.* If you get tired of hearing milk sloshing around in your stomach, just remember that this is the wonderful white stuff from which muscles grow.

In addition to drinking milk, plan to eat three large meals a day, with snacks in between. The size of your meals, as well as the size and frequency of your snacks, depends on how heavy you are to start out with and how quickly you would like to gain weight. You might begin with your three basic meals, the milk, and one snack. If your weight gains aren't satisfactory, increase your milk

---

*The first time I tried this program, I had a summer job as a construction worker. Undaunted, I kept my milk consumption on track by lugging a gallon thermos filled with milk to work every morning. I ended up gaining thirty pounds in six weeks, and after telling Peary Rader about my experience, my progress was reported in *Iron Man* (Strosser [sic], 1969).

consumption and/or your number of snacks. For both your meals and snacks, stick to basic wholesome foods: meat, fish, poultry, dairy products, eggs, whole grains, legumes, fresh fruit and vegetables. If you focus on healthful food, rather than viewing this as an excuse to just pig out on junk, you will look and feel much better as a result.

Sample Daily Diet

Here's a sample daily diet that meets the calorie and protein standards recommended for gaining weight (Bickel, 1964):

7:00 Breakfast

3 eggs
1 slice of bread
1 glass of milk

9:30 Snack

1/2 sandwich (meat)
1 glass of milk

12:00 Lunch

1 sandwich (meat)
1 sandwich (cheese)
1 glass of milk
1 piece of fruit

3:00 Snack

1 egg (hard-boiled)
1 slice of cheese
1 glass of milk

6:00 Supper

3/4 pound of meat

2 vegetables
2 glasses of milk
1 piece of fruit

9:00 Snack

1/4 pound of cheese
2 glasses of milk

This diet provides approximately 4,750 calories and 253 grams of protein and provides an example of what has been used very successfully along with the 20-rep squat program. Modify this diet to meet your needs—adding, subtracting, or changing items as necessary.

The first thing you might notice about this diet is the sheer quantity of food consumed, but remember that this approach was developed before the days of food supplements, so it took a lot of food to supply the target levels of calories and protein. Actually, many diets of this type were quite a bit heavier than this one, easily adding, for example, to the above breakfast: a glass of orange juice, a bowl of cooked cereal, some ham or bacon, and probably another egg and glass of milk while you were at it.

The second thing you might notice about this diet is that it contains a lot of cholesterol, which you might view as an expressway to arteriosclerosis or atherosclerosis. As with the knee issue, if you have any doubts, please check with your family physician, but be aware that the cholesterol issue is hardly one-sided—despite what you might have been reading in magazines at the grocery store checkout line.

Nearly twenty-five years ago a leading nutritionist pointed out that, "Cholesterol is merely the innocent little pig who got stuck in the barn door" (Davis, 1965, p. 48), meaning that an undersupply of the nutrients for using fats, rather than the mere presence of fats, is the real dietary issue. The same source also stated that three fatty acids (linoleic, linolenic, and arachidonic) common to vegetable oils are essential for cholesterol utilization. Even more telling in terms of casting the purportedly villainous cholesterol in a different light is the citation of research going back to 1935. This research showed that "experimental heart disease, produced by feeding cholesterol, could be prevented merely by giving a small amount of lecithin" (Davis, 1965, p. 50). Interestingly, even though this dietary pattern (and the need for exercise) is still acknowledged by contemporary nutritional researchers (cf., e.g., Kirschmann and Dunne, 1984), it has yet to be absorbed by the cholesterol-phobic general public, which has been well-indoctrinated with what has been dubbed, "the *Reader's Digest* view of coronary thrombosis" (Gironda, 1976, p. 17; Grace, 1977, p. 23).

As protein supplements became more common, they began to figure more prominently in weight-gaining diets, usually showing up for the scheduled snacks. It also became common for trainees to mix up their favorite blender bomb, usually based on milk, lots of powdered milk, and a banana. These basics allowed the average trainee to enjoy the benefits of commercial protein supplements at a fraction of their cost. Building on this foundation, everyone usually developed a preferred formula, and there were many that could probably have packed muscle on a grasshopper.

As an example of what else might go into these high-octane concoctions, consider the following possibilities: pineapple, peaches, coconut, ice cream, honey, blackstrap molasses, nutritional (brewer's) yeast, soy flour, peanut butter, desiccated liver, lecithin, wheat germ oil, sunflower oil, safflower oil, peanut oil, eggs (raw for the traditionalist and soft-boiled for the hardcore trainee), tuna, and the kitchen sink, if you still have room in your blender. Here's an example of a classic, albeit basic, blender bomb:

4 cups of whole milk
2 cups of powdered milk
1/4 cup of nutritional (brewer's) yeast
1 banana
2 tablespoons of lecithin
1 tablespoon of wheat germ oil
1 large scoop of vanilla ice cream

This little beast packs around 100 grams of high quality protein to the quart, along with enough calories to more than offset the trouble of making it. Drink one of these a day, eat lots of good food, do the squats, get plenty of rest, and in six weeks you will grow so much that your mother won't recognize you.

Regardless of exactly what your daily diet looks like, you are wasting your time on the *Super Squats* program if it doesn't follow the general guidelines presented above. Hise never gained until he switched to a high-protein diet, including plenty of meat (Hise, 1940b). He felt, "The most important thing in training is food—lots of it and plenty of protein," and recommended two or three pounds of meat a day (Hise, 1938).

Supplements

Food supplements are conspicuously absent from the diet presented above. *Super Squats* doesn't imply that food supplements don't work; rather, it relies upon a nutritional program that simply uses food from the grocery store. If you would like to, go ahead and augment this basic diet with all the food supplements you can afford—start with vitamin and mineral supplements, go to protein supplements next, and finally include any of the other items you would like to try.

Sources of performance-oriented nutritional advice abound, but Jerry Brainum and Dr. Frederick C. Hatfield are two authors who have consistently proven helpful. Jerry Brainum is a regular contributor to the leading body-building magazines (e.g., Brainum, 1987a,b). He has plenty of hands-on bodybuilding experience, and writes in a very digestible style. He always appears to have done his homework, slices through the confusion surrounding many of the hot topics in nutrition today, and seems committed to presenting a balanced view. This last point is very important in an age where many, if not most, so-called nutrition experts are in the business of selling supplements along with their advice. Perhaps one of the best indicators of Jerry Brainum's nutritional expertise is the fact that many of the top professional bodybuilders seek out his advice (Balik, 1988).

Dr. Hatfield also writes for the leading Iron Game publications, and has compiled his thoughts on nutrition in several books (e.g., Hatfield, 1987). A contemporary powerlifter, "Dr. Squat" has proven himself fully worthy of his nickname by squatting 1,014 pounds (Lambert, 1988)—not too shabby for a guy in his mid-forties who weighed well under 300 pounds! It would probably be hard to find a better combination of nutritional knowledge and squatting proficiency in one body, so lend him an ear if you want to learn more about food supplements.

Rest

Exercise stimulates growth by tearing down the muscles, setting the stage for their repair—in a larger, stronger form. Such recuperation depends on two other factors: diet and rest. Diet, as outlined above, provides the raw materials (that is, the natural resources) capable of being transformed into more massive muscles. The regenerative process also requires adequate rest, in the form of both sleep and relaxation. Thus diet provides the substance for rebuilding the body, and rest is the process that allows the material to be put to good use.

The cycle of exercising-eating-resting defines the principal elements in the muscle-building equation. Too much exercise or inadequate nutrition/rest will actually reduce your muscular mass and strength. An overabundance of nutrition/rest will lead to excess fat or a muscular growth rate below what is possible. Try to keep both sides of the muscle-building equation in balance, but err on the side of oversupplying the restoration factors. Thus, as with diet, when you are bulking up it's better to get too much rest and relaxation. Sleep at least eight hours a night and:

> . . . don't stand when you can sit—don't run when you can walk and don't sit when you can lie down. In other words, work very hard on your workouts but do as little as possible between them. Extra work will defeat your purpose (Rader, 1964, p. 71).

Didn't you always secretly envy couch potatoes?

John McCallum refers to this process as "softening up":

> The fat cat life feels pretty good once in a while. And the change, strangely, will do you a world of good . . . Once you decide to give the routine an honest try, you can figure on a few nice things happening to you. You can plan on a tremendous surge in your energy supply, greatly increased training enthusiasm, a whole new outlook on living, and, most of all, a big boost in your bodyweight (McCallum, 1970a).

And don't think this need to get enough rest is merely an unnecessary modern twist to our time-honored program: The venerable J. C. Hise advised twenty-one or twenty-two hours of leisure per day for top results (Hise, 1938). Nice if you can swing it.

When you are in a hurry to get big and strong, taking it easy is often the hardest thing in the world, even when you understand intellectually that progress requires adequate rest. When you are dying to attack the weights, but rest is on the schedule, try to put your energy on hold: Getting fully recovered for an especially intense assault on the bar-bells during your next workout is the best thing you can do for your progress. Go dream about your greatness, read a book or see a movie instead of sneaking into the gym ahead of schedule.

Attitude

"Conceive, believe, achieve," is the advice of super-strongman Bill Kazmaier (Ciola, 1987). Your actions are best directed toward a specific target, so conceive one. Be-gin with a general image of what you would like to look like, feel like, be capable of. Let your mind wander, and use your imagination to picture yourself evolving. What do you look like with another fifteen pounds of muscle? How do you feel? What can you do that you can't do now?

To make this program work, you have to believe in it. Use the self-images you just developed to reinforce your belief and your motivation, as well as to set short-range goals (for example, following the program, with the objec-tive of gaining at least ten pounds in the first month). Now that you know where you're headed, it's time to put your program in gear, time to begin achieving your goals, time to act.

Action is the acid test of your motivation, which in turn rests on your conception of your goal and your belief in this goal and your ability to reach it. Don't short-change the power of positive beliefs by dismissing them as some untested murky notion, or as something that helps nitwits overcome their daily obstacles. Hard-nosed, leading-edge scientists, backed up by research in the most prestigious psychology laboratories, have outlined the theoretical un-derpinnings of belief systems, and have described and doc-umented their undeniable influence on what we do and our chances of success (Bandura, 1977). You are what you believe.

Keep on track by believing in yourself (you know you can do it), sticking with your exercise program (gutting out those squats with an added five or ten pounds each workout), following your diet (adhering to your protein-caloric content guidelines), and resting as you should. To paraphrase Muhammad Ali: To be a champion, you have to believe you are great and if you can't do that, at least fake it.

So what are you waiting for? "Breathing squats have resulted in fabulous gains in the past and they can do it for you, too" (Rader, 1963, p. 56).

5 The Finer Points

[John McCallum's friend, Ollie, is quizzing the maestro about the near-flawless record of the squat program.]
"It seems to me there ought to be the odd failure."
"Look," I said. "Any time anybody fails on squats, it's their own fault. They're doing something wrong" (McCallum, 1969, p. 11).

To keep you from making a mistake, we have hammered on the basics over and over: Squat in good form, use heavy weights with lots of breathing, and add weight every workout; eat lots of high-protein foods and drink plenty of milk; rest and relax as much as you can; and maintain a positive outlook. So much for the basics. What are some of the finer points that could speed up your progress?

Medium-Tech Options for Squatting

The philosophy of this program has been pretty low-tech, emphasizing basic equipment, exercises, and food. To round out the picture on *Super Squats*, however, we'll describe three higher-tech alternatives for those who simply cannot, or prefer not to, do traditional barbell squats.

The first alternative involves using a cambered bar and was invented by J. C. Hise (Howell, 1978). The second involves using a so-called "Magic Circle," and was invented by James E. Douglass, who probably knew J. C. Hise about as well as anyone outside of Mr. Hise's hometown of Homer, Illinois (Douglass, 1988a). The third alternative employs a hip belt, was introduced by the venerable Charles A. Ramsey (Hise, 1940b), and has been most seriously used in recent times by John McCallum (McCallum, 1970c). Thus each of these alternatives to using the straight bar for squats has the sort of thoroughbred heritage to merit its consideration. Let's see what they have to offer.

When he was getting ready to work out one day, J. C. Hise found that his brother had bent his bar while working on his Model T: Straightening it out, Joe resumed his workout only to have the inspiration to rebend the bar as a way to reduce the discomfort of having the bar cut into and roll around on the back of his neck (Howell, 1978). Thus was born the cambered squat bar, which used to be a staple for heavy squatting. Do-it-yourselfers were advised simply to buy a bar of the right diameter and length from their hardware store and bend it, putting in about a one-inch camber (Rader, 1956a).* For whatever reason, cambered bars are rarely seen anymore, but they remain an excellent alternative to straight bars for doing heavy squats. Incidentally, although still short of using a true cambered bar, your squatting comfort will increase dramatically if you use a high-quality lifting bar, which will naturally drape across your shoulders under the load of your squatting poundage.

The Magic Circle began life as the "Douglass Harness,"** a rectangular frame supported over the shoulders by straps and loaded with weights (Douglass, 1954). The purpose of the Douglass Harness was to solve the problem

---

*Chester O. Teegarden used to make the Rolls-Royce of cambered bars: He bent a 7 1/2-foot length of 1 3/4-inch round steel bar in five places to produce a 4-inch arc. One foot on either end of the bar was turned down to 1 1/16 inch, to fit exercise plates; and the ends were bent up to keep the plates on a level bar without requiring collars. The bar was balanced and weighed 50 pounds when finished (Teegarden, 1988b).

**J. C. Hise dubbed his friend's invention the "Hula Hoop," which is also how Jim Douglass refers to it (Douglass, 1988b, p. 2).

of traditional squats hunching the shoulders forward, as well as to reduce the discomfort of supporting heavy weights on one's shoulders. James Douglass went on to refine his invention by making an improved model in the form of a circle (Douglass, 1954) and the design was sold for decades by Peary Rader's Body Culture Equipment Company under the name of the "Magic Circle." Like the cambered squat bar, the Magic Circle seems to have fallen from favor, but not for its inability to produce results:

> In 1964 this device (The Magic Circle) was made available to readers of *Iron Man* and since then has proven the most popular piece of equipment other than the barbell. Many readers have reported greatly accelerated progress because they could work harder with more weight and with almost no discomfort. For many men the Magic Circle became the No. 1 piece of training equipment. (Rader, 1968, p. 28)

Diehard traditionalists contemplating squatting with a Magic Circle will be happy to know that J. C. Hise used one personally made for him by James E. Douglass (Roark, 1986), and that Hise considered it "the best invention ever" for these breathing squats (Douglass, 1988b, p. 3).

The hip belt squat was Charles A. Ramsey's solution to allow his pupils with "glass backs" to gain the benefits of squatting (Hise, 1940b, p. 13). John McCallum has called hip belt squats "*the absolute best* for bulking your lower thighs" (McCallum, 1963, p. 48). He later developed a program based on the exercise that produced "terrific results" for everybody who tried it (McCallum, 1970c, p. 44).

As the name implies, this approach to squatting involves hanging the barbell from a chain or rope attached to a heavy belt around one's waist: Without any weight on one's shoulders, it's easier to breath really deeply, and by putting a block of wood under one's heels, the workload can be concentrated on the muscles just above the knee.* In McCallum's well-publicized experiment with his hip squat routine (McCallum, 1970c), one formerly anonymous and very ordinary Henry Masters gained twenty-six pounds in two months, putting almost two inches on his arms and boosting his deadlift nearly 50 percent. Not too bad—especially for a guy who had been training for about a year and a half, but had never "gained an ounce" before this routine (McCallum, 1970c, p. 44). If you still need to be convinced that hip belt squats are a worthy variant on the basic barbell squat theme, just remember that they were John McCallum's personal favorite when he was transforming his body from a bag of bones to a Herculean structure (Rader, 1967).

Even if you have always thrived on traditional barbell squats, using one or more of these alternatives could prove to be a refreshing and productive variant.

Goals: Bodyweight, Size, and Strength

Without a goal, you will probably waste a lot of time casting about for who knows what. Armed with a goal, you can set a course, make corrections as necessary, and—most important—gain some satisfaction from knowing when you've arrived. Let's talk about some of the basic goals related to this program.

Bodyweight

Let's start with bodyweight, since it is the primary determinant of your relative appearance and strength. The first thing to remember is that the so-called normal

---

*The details of making and using a hip belt are beyond the scope of *Super Squats*, but anyone interested in trying the exercise should be able to rig up a suitable belt at almost no cost. For a detailed explanation, see McCallum, 1970b.

weights advised by your physician or life insurance agent will bear little resemblance to what a strong, well-developed person will weigh. The second point is that a given bodyweight is no guarantee of a particular level of size or strength—so treat the bathroom scale as a guide, not an absolute rule, letting your appearance and performance help you interpret what you read on the dial.

What's a good rule of thumb to use for your bodyweight if you are aiming for a strong, well-developed body? As a general guideline for bodyweight, when you're talking about being well-developed and strong, consider the following system (Brown, 1967): Starting with a height of 5'0", take 100 pounds as your basic bodyweight. Add or subtract 10 pounds for each inch over or under 5 feet in height. Thus, for example, the basic weight guideline for someone who is 5'11" would be 210 pounds: 100 pounds + (11 × 10 pounds). In terms of a general idea of what your maximum muscular bodyweight is, add 30 or 40 pounds to your basic bodyweight. Using this formula, a man 6'0" would have a basic bodyweight of 220 pounds and a maximum muscular bodyweight of between 250 and 260 pounds.

Remember that these are only guidelines—not hard-and-fast rules. Shorter people will generally have to weigh more relatively (that is, get closer to their maximum) than taller people to look as impressive; and smaller-boned people will have more trouble hitting a projected maximum muscular bodyweight than will someone with heavy bones (often settling for, say, 15 to 30 pounds less muscle than their heavily boned counterparts).

Whether you are tall or short, slender-framed or massive, aiming for your basic or maximum muscular bodyweight, chances are good that if you haven't been on a productive bodybuilding program for some time already, you have plenty of room for adding piles of muscles to your frame. Get growing.

Size

Reading the purported measurements of contemporary bodybuilders is likely to leave you with the impression that they all have 21-inch arms, 53-inch chests, 30-inch waists, and everything else in proportion. Of course, most of the reported measurements bear little resemblance to the facts (McCallum, 1964, Roark, 1987), so they can do little more than mislead, confuse, and frustrate most people who look to them for guidelines in terms of defining obtainable levels of muscular development.

What are some guidelines for honest, realistic measurements?* John McCallum (1964) has presented a formula for calculating some goals you can use to guide your program. Start off with an accurate tape and measure your wrist (just above the protruding bone) to obtain a good idea of your bone size and you're all set:

1. Multiply your wrist measurement by 6.5 and you have a reasonable idea of what your chest can measure. Since your chest is a governing factor in your overall muscular mass, this measurement becomes the starting point for calculating all your other measurements.
2. Grant yourself 70 percent of this chest measurement for your waist and 85 percent for your hips.
3. Shoot for 36 percent for your upper arm and 29 percent for your forearm.
4. Take 53 percent for your thighs and 34 percent for your calves.
5. Top it off with 37 percent for your neck.

---

*Notably, in addition to providing an indication of what one might honestly attain in terms of muscular size, these guidelines also expressly provide a glimpse at the wondrous results available without drugs, life-consuming routines, exotic equipment, or bizarre diets.

Using this system a man with a 7-inch wrist (indicating fairly small bones) would measure as follows: chest 45.5 inches, waist 31.9 inches, arm 16.4 inches, forearm 13.2 inches, hips 38.7 inches, thigh 24.1 inches, calf 15.5 inches, and neck 16.8 inches. Similarly, a man with an 8-inch wrist (indicating quite large bones) would measure as follows: chest 52 inches, waist 36.4 inches, arm 18.7 inches, forearm 15 inches, hips 44.2 inches, thigh 27.6 inches, calf 17.7 inches, and neck 19.2 inches. People with larger or smaller bones would have their measurements adjusted accordingly, up or down.

Above all, always remember two things about measurements. First, like bodyweight, don't confuse the means with the end—believe the mirror and how you feel and perform more than what the tape says. Second, since you might have never run into a single set of honest measurements in your life, don't think the above guides are ridiculously conservative—achieve something on their order of magnitude and you'll have a physique you can be proud of anywhere.

Strength

Just how strong can you get? How much weight will you be lifting if you are working as hard on this program as you should be? What sort of poundages are you going to be hoisting to achieve a Herculean physique?

The squat, of course, is the cornerstone of your efforts to get big and strong, so you practically need look no further than to how much weight you are handling for your twenty reps of knee bends. You might be intimidated to learn that 150 percent of bodyweight is a good *minimum* figure for anyone who is really serious about gaining (McCallum, 1968). Remember the story about how Peary Rader started off with only a bit more than the empty bar and went on to break this standard? You can do this too if you only follow the program and work hard enough.

The squat is the basic exercise, but to help you understand your strength goals here are a couple more suggestions: Aim for at least 75 percent of your bodyweight for twelve reps in the press behind the neck—that's a lot, but you'll get shoulders, arms, and an upper back like you never imagined if you make this goal (McCallum, 1968). Need a few more? Aim for at least 125 percent of your bodyweight in strict bent-over rows for a dozen reps, about the same for your bench presses, and try to keep your stiff-legged deadlift poundage even with your squats. Once you hit all these training weights, you should have strength to spare in any task you'll ever encounter and, if you wish, you can really dig in and find out just how strong you can become.

By now it should be clear that there's no point in trying to build up your body unless you're willing to get powerful at the same time. And to get strong you *must* lift heavy weights. It's really just that simple.

Record Keeping

Even if you can accept in principle the idea of setting goals and working steadily to achieve them, you might not automatically recognize how important it is to continually track your progress.

One reason productive weight training is so satisfying is that, along with all the hidden benefits, your gains are right out in the open—your once-skinny arms now fill your sleeves, you can do repetition curls with a barbell you were unable to roll across the floor a few months ago, and so on. The big advantage of the gains, from a tracking perspective, is that they are easy to measure.

First, weigh yourself and take all your measurements at the beginning of your program—be sure to write down the results and don't cheat yourself by lying about what the tape and scale read. Second, set up a training log and record every single lift on every single workout. Third, check your weight and your measurements at regular intervals. Take the time to review your training poundages periodically. Fourth, if you really want some powerful visual evidence of your progress, take photos of yourself at the start of your program and at key intervals thereafter, and plot some of your key training poundages on graph paper. If you're working as hard as you should be, this last step will knock your socks off.

Most people are in the habit of weighing themselves regularly, so that's usually not a problem—just be sure to write down your results so you can monitor your progress. Also, once you start training, you probably will rarely stray more than five feet from a tape measure and will be measuring your upper arm at least several times a week. Even if you don't get this nutty, tracking your key measurements seems to be automatic once you start training. The photo-taking also tends to take care of itself: The physique-conscious will probably collect lots of pictures of themselves, and those who view their physique as only a means to an end (such as improved strength and health) won't be bothered whether they have photos or not. The one area that really needs to be discussed a bit is the training log.

Performance feedback is one of the most potent forces shaping future behavior. Without it, you are just shooting in the dark. The purpose of maintaining a training diary is to give you performance feedback—it documents where you have been, providing both information and reinforcement to help you get where you are going. For example, if you're not gaining properly and you have a training diary to review, a glance might tell you that you haven't been sticking to your workout schedule and meeting your goals for increasing your training poundages. Conversely, you'll get a very motivating sense of satisfaction from seeing that you haven't missed a single workout in six weeks, your squat weight has gone up ninety pounds in that period, and you've gained thirty pounds of solid muscle. Graphing your results is like putting your training log under a microscope. For example, it will immediately tell you whether or not you've been boosting your training poundages according to your schedule.

Don't feel this training log has to be something fancy—any simple notebook will do and ordinary stenographer pads have an illustrious history of serving in this capacity. Note the date, and list every single exercise, followed by the weight used and the number of reps performed. Repeat the weight × repetition notation for each set you do. You might also add information on your bodyweight, a general comment about how you felt and specific comments about how a given exercise felt. For example, your log might look like this:

November 8, 1988 Felt great — weighed 172 in am
Press behind the neck   120 × 12 , 120 × 12
Bench press 180×12, 180×12 arched on last rep
Bent over rows 135 × 12 , 135×12
Squat   245×20 hard but solid!
Pullovers   25 × 20
Stiff legged deadlift 245×17 lost grip-lots of pull left
Pullovers   25×20
Leg raises 25

As you can see, each exercise is followed by the weight used and the number of reps performed, repeated for each set. Where relevant, a specific comment was written down—it might be explanatory or reinforcing, whatever is appropriate. Maintaining and studying your training log is one of the most productive adjuncts to following your basic exercise-diet-rest regimen, but it's a training tool that is all too often overlooked or underutilized. Information is power. So remember that your log provides you the information necessary to boost your power.

Getting Psyched

Throughout *Super Squats* you have been advised to work beyond your customary limits, to use your mind to will your body to new heights. It's time to introduce a specific tool to help you do just that. The fundamental approach we are going to employ has gone by many different names, but let's keep things simple and descriptive and merely call it "mental rehearsal."

Although nearly miraculous, this technique warrants two cautionary notes. First, the whole mental rehearsal process genuinely is a skill, so expect to have to put in some practice before you get up to full speed. Second, as amazing as this technique is, don't expect to apply it simultaneously to half a dozen areas—stick to one at a time. On this program you would be hard pressed to find a more productive application than keeping your squat poundage rolling up and up and up. Later on, you can apply it to remake virtually any portion of your attitudinal or behavioral repertoire.

Let's lay some groundwork for this skill. One way we can really use our heads in training is to picture our success—creating what we would like to have happen in our minds, so that it becomes easier for our bodies to follow. Here's how it works.

First, we are going to learn how to achieve a very deep state of relaxation—this will set the stage for imagining what we choose. Second, down to the most minute detail and across all the senses we can invoke, we are going to picture a scene as we would like it to unfold. Third, we are going to run through this many times before we actually face the critical task. Fourth, just before we finally face the critical task, we are going to run through one last mental rehearsal of our successful performance. Fifth, we're going to actually do it. It's not as complicated as it sounds, and the results are just short of miraculous.

Without going into all the reasons why, our success with mental rehearsal will be greatly enhanced if we first achieve a state of deep relaxation. There are many ways to reach this goal, but they can be defined in terms of three basic techniques: (1) deep breathing, (2) progressive relaxation, and (3) autogenic training. Let's briefly review each of these techniques and then put together a program of mental training that can make your training poundages zoom upward.

Deep breathing is pretty much what it sounds like. Take slow, deep breaths that fill your diaphragm with air—don't just fill your upper lungs. To check whether you are properly filling your diaphragm for this deep-breathing technique, lie on your back and take a few breaths. If your belly is stationary and your chest rises and falls with your breaths, you aren't breathing correctly—make your belly rise and fall as you breathe.

Progressive relaxation involves systematically tensing and relaxing your muscles (Jacobson, 1938). The idea here is that muscular tension and relaxation are incompatible, and the two need to be distinguished. The best way to do this, and thereby achieve deep relaxation, is alternately to tense and relax the muscles.

Autogenic training is very commonly used by Eastern European athletes (Garfield and Bennett, 1985). It allows one to control a surprisingly wide range of internal functions—including many that had formerly been thought to be under involuntary control (such as heart rate). Our application of autogenic training is not going to push the technique to its limits; rather, we will use it to teach our bodies to relax in response to verbal cues.

Some people respond better to one of these techniques than to others. So, to optimize your relaxation response, our recommended approach draws upon all three.

To begin this relaxation exercise, pick a quiet spot where you can lie down, where you will be comfortably warm, and where you will not be disturbed: It might be a park, the beach, or your bedroom. Your clothing should be loose—no tight belts or collars, and removing your shoes is a good idea. Other than your breathing, you should try to remain motionless throughout this entire exercise, so it's important to get comfortable from the outset.

Lie on your back without crossing your legs. Keep your arms by your side or cross your hands lightly over your waist. Even though you aren't going to sleep, it is helpful to allow your eyes to close. Take a few slow, deep breaths, ensuring that they make your stomach rise and fall. Breathe in through your nose and out through your mouth. As you inhale picture a soothing but strong wave covering your body like a blanket; and as you exhale picture all the stress, tension, and worries you might have drifting off into space. Take at least three or four breaths like this. Then roll your head around slowly, shrug your shoulders gently, and make a couple of faces, crunching up your facial muscles and then releasing them. Now just relax. These exercises pinpoint some of the most frequent sites of tension and should help you let it evaporate.

You should begin to feel more relaxed now; remember, your relaxation skills will improve with practice. Next, move to your toes and feet—tense the muscles, hold the tension for a second, and then let it go. Pause for a second or two and do the same thing with your calves—tense the muscles, hold the tension for a second, and then let it go. Pause again and move to your thighs. Repeat this same process through your hips, stomach, chest and back, shoulders and upper back, neck, and finally your face. Be careful not to tense your muscles to the point of cramping when you do this exercise—just tense them enough to get a clear idea of the sensation and then let go.

Take two or three deep breaths—just as you did at the very beginning of this exercise. Now you should feel noticeably more relaxed than when you began, but we are going through one more stage to take you into an even deeper level of relaxation. Start with your right leg and say, "My right leg is warm and heavy. I am relaxed." Repeat this to yourself five times and do the same thing with your left leg. Do the same thing with your right arm and then your left arm. Finally, repeat this message five times: "My whole body is warm and heavy. I am relaxed."

By now you should have the sensation of being alert, but without any direct feeling from your body. You are now primed to begin mentally rehearsing the scenes of your success!

Let's walk through a mental rehearsal of successful squatting. Remember: This same technique can be applied to virtually any aspect of your life. Picture your gym—create the image in as much detail as you can. What does it look like? Familiar smells? Sounds? Textures? Imagine the bar loaded to the exact weight you want to squat—mentally loading the bar can help you form a sharp image. Stare at the bar and get under it. Don't be afraid to admit that it's heavy—it is, but you're lifting it and gaining some self-confidence from the way you are mastering it. One by one, knock off each of the reps you plan to do with the weight—feel each one and don't cheat by skipping any! When you've finished the set, put the bar back and give yourself some verbal pats on the back. *Nice set!*

Go through this drill at least twice before a training session—at night, lying in bed just before going to sleep, is a convenient time to do this mental training. In the gym, right before you actually knock off the set, find a quiet corner and sit down for a couple of minutes and walk through an abbreviated version of this mental rehearsal exercise. If you can't block out the distractions around you, drape a towel over your head—this might look funny, but it works and nobody is going to laugh at your results. Immediately after finishing this final drill, go do the real thing and you'll be amazed at how powerful you've become: After being stuck for months at 430 pounds for three reps in the squat, John McCallum applied this basic system and cranked out three full reps with 500 pounds (McCallum, 1965). And you thought this mental rehearsal stuff was just a lot of hooey.

Absolutely nothing can stop you now.

Afterword

I started Marvin on weights a couple of years ago on a bet. It was a mistake. He got to like it. Marvin's training methods are as simple as he is. He went from a skinny nut to a bulky nut in nothing flat by squatting three times a week and eating everything that didn't bite back.

Marvin avoids work like the bubonic plague. His only other recreation is the beach. He walks around with his chest stuck out, eats hamburgers, and kicks sand in everyone's face (McCallum, 1968a, p. 13).*

If Marvin could get big and strong, so can you—but be prepared for the results. Following this program will tend to put you in the spotlight: You are going to start to look like someone with muscles, because you are going to build some. Not everyone will end up looking like John Grimek or Arnold Schwarzenegger, but everyone can built a body that's more than impressive, and the results are going to show in a lot of ways.

All this progress, all this new-found muscle mass and power, should be able to carry a small new responsibility: that of being modest about your might. For decades sound bodybuilding programs were known by their practitioners to provide enormous benefits to one's development, strength, health, and outlook. Unfortunately one of the things that worked against the public's widespread accep-

---

*True McCallumites will recognize that this quotation is taken out of context, but—with due apologies to Marvin and John—it illustrated our point too well to pass up.

tance of weight training was the tendency of a few bodybuilders to be showoffs ("lat spreaders") or worse, bullies.
As a small price to pay in return for all that weight training
gave you, recognize that you are now a public relations
agent for the Iron Game (McCallum, 1966) and conduct
yourself in a manner worthy of the activity that allowed
you to completely retool yourself, from the inside out. End
of lecture.

References*

Anderson, P. Squatting for Power. *Muscular Development 1*, Number 11 (November 1964): 20–22 ff.

Balik, J. Editorial: Arnold's Secrets. *IRONMAN 47*, Number 7 (July 1988): 7.

Bandura, A. Self-Efficacy: Toward a Unifying Theory of Behavioral Change. *Psychological Review 84*, Number 2 (March 1977): 191–215.

Benjamin, R. The Deadlift (from the series "Foundation Training"). *Powerlifting USA 6*, Number 12 (June 1983): 36–37.

Berry, M. H. Chest Improvement Through Vigorous Leg Exercise. *The Strong Man 1*, Number 5 (October 1931): 18–19 ff.

Berry, M. H. One Reader. *The Strong Man 2*, Number 3 (February 1932):45. (a)

Berry, M. H. An Idea Worth Trying In Body Building. *The Arena and Strength 17*, Number 5 (August 1932): 16–19 ff. (b)

Berry, M. H. If You Are Looking For Secrets. *The Arena and Strength 17*, Number 12 (March 1933):14–17 ff. (a)

Berry, M. H. Specialized Improvement Measures Outlined. *The Arena and Strength 18*, Number 2 (May 1933): 14–17 ff. (b)

Berry, M. H. Found—A Growing Exercise. *The Arena and Strength 18*, Number 3 (June 1933): 14–17 ff. (c)

---

*Two comments are in order regarding citations of the magazine *Iron Man*. First, the earliest issues bore no publication dates, since they came out at irregular intervals. In cases where such issues are cited, the publication date was estimated and is indicated as such (e.g., circa 1937). Second, when John Balik bought the magazine from Peary Rader in late 1986, he changed the logo from *Iron Man* to *IRONMAN*.

Berry, M. H. Right and Wrong Methods. *The Arena and Strength 18*, Number 5 (August 1933): 13–16 ff. (d)

Berry, M. H. I'll Do Anything To Gain Weight. *The Arena and Strength 19*, Number 1 (April 1934): 11–14 ff.

Bickel, V. Maximum Nutrition for Maximum Muscular Gains. *Iron Man 23*, Number 3 (January–February 1964):16–17 ff.

Brainum, J. Ergogenics (Part I). *IRONMAN 46*, Number 6 (September 1987):42–45. (a)

Brainum, J. Ergogenics (Part II). *IRONMAN 47*, Number 1 (November 1987): 60–63. (b)

Brainum, J. Pec Perfection. *IRONMAN 47*, Number 10 (October 1988): 112–118 ff.

Brown, B. What Should You Weigh? (As told to Peary Rader.) *Iron Man 26*, Number 3 (March 1967): 30–32 ff.

Charles, D. Powerhouse Thighs. *IRONMAN 47*, Number 6 (June 1988): 36–40 ff.

Ciola, T. Bill Kazmaier—Rapping with One of the World's Strongest Men. *Iron Man 46*, Number 1 (October–November 1986): 54 ff.

Cleveland, G. Mel Hennesy [sic]—Super Bodybuilder. *Strength & Health 34*, Number 3 (March 1966): 28–29 ff.

Coyle, R. Squats: The Natural Maxibolic (Part I). *IRONMAN 47*, Number 11 (November 1988): 61–62.

Davis, A. *Let's Get Well.* New York: Harcourt, Brace & World, Inc., 1965.

Douglass, J. [E.] More About the Douglass Harness. *Iron Man 14*, Number 2 (August–September 1954): 36 ff.

Douglass, J. E. Personal communication, May 18, 1988. (a)

Douglass, J. E. Personal communication, August 9, 1988. (b)

Draper, D. *Get Serious!!*, Capitola, CA: On Target With Dave Draper, 1988.

Drummond, M. Association Notes. *The Arena and Strength 18*, Number 11 (February 1934): 36–38 ff. (a)

Drummond, M. Association Notes. *The Arena and Strength 19*, Number 4 (August 1934): 41–43 ff. (b)

Eells, R. G. *A Larger More Shapely Chest Can Be Yours.* Roger Eells, 1940. (a)

Eells, R. [G.] Specialization. *Vim 1*, Number 6 (July 1940): 5 ff. (b)

Garfield, C. A. and H. Z. Bennett. *Peak Performance*. New York: Warner Books, Inc., 1985.

Gironda, V. In Defense of Cholesterol. *Iron Man 35*, Number 5 (June–July 1976): 17 ff.

Glossbrenner, H. History's Strongest Man: The Story of Paul Anderson. *IRONMAN 46*, Number 5 (July 1987): 18 ff.

Grace, F. In Defense of Cholesterol. *Iron Man 36*, Number 5 (June–July 1977): 23 ff.

Grimek, J. C. Yesterday & Today—George Jowett: Strength Pioneer. *IRONMAN 47*, Number 5 (May 1988): 104–107.

Hatfield, F. C. *Ultimate Sports Nutrition*. Chicago: Contemporary Books, Inc., 1987.

Hepburn, D. Body Power: How to Develop It. *Iron Man 21*, Number 1 (August–September 1961): 29 ff.

Herrick, R. T., M. Stone, and S. Herrick. Knee Injuries of Strength–Power Athletes. *IRONSPORT 1*, Number 1 (March/April 1987): 41–43.

Hise, J. C. Strong Men Made Easy (Part I). *Iron Man 2*, Number 2 (circa 1937): 6–8. (a)

Hise, J. C. Strong Men Made Easy (Part II). *Iron Man 2*, Number 3 (circa 1937): 11–15. (b)

Hise, J. C. The Secret of Superb Physical Development. *The Weight-Lifter* (Jim Evans, Editor), special issue (circa 1938).

Hise, J. C. Shapeliness Simplified. *Vim 1*, Number 6 (July 1940): 12 ff. (a)

Hise, J. C. The Value of the Squat. *Vim 1*, Number 9 (October 1940): 12–15 ff. (b)

Hise, J. C. The Value of the Squat (continued). *Vim 1*, Number 11 (November 1940): 12–15 ff. (c)

Hise, J. C. Gains, Gaining and Gainers. *Vim 2*, Number 5 (May 1941): 16–17 ff.

Howell, F. R. The Hise Shoulder Shrug. *Iron Man 26*, Number 4 (April–May 1967): 24 ff.

Howell, F. [R.] Joseph C. Hise—Pioneer of Power Lifting. *Iron Man 37*, Number 4 (May 1978): 32–33 ff.

Howell, F. R. The Mysterious Hise Shrug. *Iron Man 46*, Number 1 (November 1986): 44–45 ff.

Howell, F. R. Personal communication, March 27, 1988. (a)

Howell, F. R. Personal communication, May 26, 1988. (b)

Jackson, A. W. Personal communication, September 10, 1988.

Jacobson, E. *Progressive Relaxation.* Chicago: University of Chicago Press, 1938.

Kallos, A. Breathing Squat Program for Fabulous Gains. *Iron Man 22,* Number 6 (July–August 1963): 16–17 ff.

Kennedy, R. *BEEF IT! Upping the Muscle Mass.* New York: Sterling Publishing Co. Inc., 1983.

Kirschmann, J. D. and L. J. Dunne. *Nutrition Almanac ,* 2d ed. New York: McGraw-Hill Book Company, 1984.

Klein, S. The Heavy Deep-Knee Bend: How it Began. *Muscular Development 1,* Number 10 (October 1964): 23 ff.

Lambert, E. J. Top 100 275's. *Powerlifting USA 11,* Number 6 (January 1988): 41.

Lawson, L. Paul Anderson: Modern Superman—And How He Trains. *Iron Man 15,* Number 5 (February–March 1956): 10–14 ff.

Leistner, K. More from Ken Leistner. *Powerlifting USA 11,* Number 10 (May 1988): 27.

McCallum, J. Leg Specialization for Bulk. *Strength & Health* (September 1963): 24–25 ff.

McCallum, J. Your Measurements. *Strength & Health 32,* Number 12 (November 1964): 12–13 ff.

McCallum, J. Concentration—Part III (from the "Keys to Progress" series). *Strength & Health 33,* Number 9 (September 1965): 12–15 ff.

McCallum, J. Public Relations (from the "Keys to Progress" series). *Strength & Health 34,* Number 3 (March 1966): 12–13 ff.

McCallum, J. Parallel Bar Dips (from the "Keys to Progress" series). *Strength & Health 35,* Number 6 (June 1967): 14–15 ff. (a)

McCallum, J. The Basic Exercises—Part I (from the "Keys to Progress" series). *Strength & Health 35,* Number 8 (August 1967): 14–15 ff. (b)

McCallum, J. Trimming Down (from the "Keys to Progress" series). *Strength & Health 36,* Number 2 (February 1968): 12–13 ff. (a)

McCallum, J. Bulking Up (from the "Keys to Progress" series). *Strength & Health 36,* Number 11 (November 1968): 12–13 ff. (b)

McCallum, J. The Right Way (from the "Keys to Progress" series). *Strength & Health 37,* Number 1 (January 1969): 10–11 ff.

McCallum, J. Softening Up for Gains—III (from the "Keys to Progress" series). *Strength & Health* (February 1970): 56–57 ff. (a)

McCallum, J. Hip Belt Squats (from the "Keys to Progress" series). *Strength & Health 38,* Number 3 (March 1970): 50–51 ff. (b)

McCallum, J. The Hip Belt Squat Routine (from the "Keys to Progress" series). *Strength & Health 38,* Number 4 (April 1970): 44–45 ff. (c)

McCallum, J. Gain Weight to Build Your Arms—Part IV (from the "Keys to Progress" series). *Strength & Health 39,* Number 4 (April 1971): 40–41 ff.

McCallum, J. The Super Bulk and Power Thing—Part III (from the "Keys to Progress" series). *Strength & Health 40,* Number 8 (September 1972): 62–63 ff.

Page, B. The Squat—Master Exercise. *Iron Man 20,* Number 2 (September–October–November–December 1960): 34 ff.

Page, B. The Rader Chest Pull Revisited. *Iron Man 45,* Number 6 (August–September 1986): 14.

Paschall, H. B. Training for the Working Man. *Iron Man 11,* Number 6 (April–May 1952): 10–13 ff.

Paschall, H. B. The Passing Show. *Iron Man 13,* Number 5 (February–March 1954): 16–18. (a)

Paschall, H. B. The Passing Show. *Iron Man 14,* Number 3 (October–November 1954): 14–17 ff. (b)

Paschall, H. B. Strongest Man Who Ever Lived. *Iron Man 15,* Number 4 (December 1955/January 1956): 20–21 ff.

Pride, B. The Life and Death of C. A. Ramsey. *Iron Man 14,* Number 2 (August–September 1954): 34 ff.

Rader, P. A Personal Message From Your Editor. *Iron Man 2*, Number 2 (circa 1937): 3.

Rader, P. The Story of Joseph Curtis Hise. *Iron Man 3*, Number 4 (circa 1938): 4–10.

Rader, P. The Iron Man: The Deep Knee Bend Vindicated. *Iron Man 3*, Number 5 (circa 1939): 23 ff. (a)

Rader, P. Strength—Health and Development for All. *Iron Man 3*, Number 6 (circa 1939): 12–15. (b)

Rader, P. The Bodybuilders [sic] Friend—The Deep Knee Bend. *The Iron Man 4*, Number 1 (February–March 1941): 11–16.

Rader, P. Developing the Chest Through Maximum Rib Box Expansion: An Amazing New Exercise. *Iron Man 11*, Number 4 (November–December 1951): 26 ff.

Rader, P. Developing Great Strength (Your Complete Bodybuilding Program: Part Eleven). *Iron Man 13*, Number 5 (February–March 1954): 10–13 ff.

Rader, P. The Squat—Greatest Single Exercise . . . Its History, Benefits, and Performance. *Iron Man 15*, Number 1 (June–July 1955): 22–26 ff. (a)

Rader, P. Anderson Makes World Record At Senior Nationals. *Iron Man 15*, Number 2 (August–September 1955): 24–29. (b)

Rader, P. *The Rader Master Bodybuilding and Weight Gaining System.* Copyright 1946 by Peary Rader. Modernized in 1956. (a)

Rader, P. The Squat—Greatest Single Exercise . . . The Master Exercise . . . A Complete Weight Gaining Course. *Iron Man 15*, Number 6 (April–May 1956): 18–23 ff. (b)

Rader, P. News Flash. *Iron Man 15*, Number 4 (December 1955/January 1956): 14. (c)

Rader, P. The Fabulous Feats of Paul Anderson. *Iron Man 20*, Number 4 (March 1961): 20–21 ff.

Rader, P. Editor's Note. *Iron Man 22*, Number 6 (July–August 1963): 54 ff.

Rader, P. Squat—Still King of Exercises. *Iron Man 24*, Number 1 (October–November–December 1964): 24–26 ff.

Rader, P. The Squat & Twenty Reps for Fast Gains—Gain a Pound a Day. *Iron Man 26*, Number 3 (March 1967): 14–15 ff.

Rader, P. How to Use the Magic Circle for Outstanding Results. *Iron Man 27*, Number 3 (March 1968): 28–30 ff.

Rader, P. Iron Man Honors Paul Anderson—A Great Man. *Iron Man 28*, Number 4 (May 1969): 12–14.

Rader, P. Personal communication, September 11, 1988.

Ramsey, C. A. Personal communication (letter to Chester O. Teegarden), November 18, 1940.

Roark, J. Untitled background article on J. C. Hise and Joe Roark interview with Glen Ellis. *The Roark Report*, Issue 8 (August/September 1986): 2–8.

Roark, J. Measurements & Malarkey. *IRONMAN 46*, Number 6 (September 1987): 117–118.

Roark, J. Personal communication, May 7, 1988.

Salvati, M. Power & Bulk Training in Your Bedroom. *Iron Man 24*, Number 1 (October–November–December 1964): 28–29.

Schwarzenegger, A. and D. K. Hall. *Arnold: The Education of a Bodybuilder*. New York: Simon and Schuster, 1979.

Smith, C. A. Personal communication, May 28, 1988. (a)

Smith, C. A. Personal communication, June 6, 1988. (b)

Stephens, H. Positive & Fast Weight Gaining. *Iron Man 23*, Number 1 (September–October 1963): 10–12 ff.

Strossen, R. J. IronMind's Intent and Purpose (from the Iron-Mind™ column). *IRONMAN 47*, Number 9 (September 1988): 74. (a)

Strossen, R. J. Overcoming Limits (from the IronMind™ column). *IRONMAN 47*, Number 10 (October 1988): 17–18.

Strosser [sic], R. J. How I gained 30 lbs. of Muscle In 6 Weeks (as told to the Editor). *Iron Man 28*, Number 2 (December 1968/January 1969): 36 ff.

Teegarden, C. O. A Superior Pullover—As Taught by C. A. Ramsey. *Iron Man 4*, Number 5 (February–March 1942): 7–8.

Teegarden, C. O. Ed. *The Training Programs of Louis Abele*, 2d ed. Lafayette, Indiana: The Strong Barbell Company, 1948.

Teegarden, C. O. Personal communication, June 18, 1988. (a)

Teegarden, C. O. Personal communication, November 15, 1988. (b)

Todd, T. *Inside Powerlifting*. Chicago: Contemporary Books, Inc., 1978.

Todd, T. Karl Klein and the Squat. *National Strength and Conditioning Association (NSCA) Journal 6*, Number 3 (June–July 1984): 26–31 ff.

Todd, T. Personal communication, February 2, 1988.

Willoughby, D. P. *The Super Athletes* . Cranbury, New Jersey: A. S. Barnes and Co., Inc., 1970.

Willoughby, D. P. Feats of Strength: Examples of Leg Strength. *Iron Man 40*, Number 2 (December 1980/January 1981): 34–35 ff.

Wright, J. This New Era. *The Arena and Strength 19*, Number 1 (April 1934): 33.

Zeller, A. The Life and Times of Reg Park. *Muscular Development 25*, Number 7 (July 1988): 22–27 ff.

Index

Ramsey, Charles A., 55, 80, 81
Recuperation, 66 ff., 75 ff.
Relaxation, 75 ff., 79, 90 ff.
Rest, *see* Recuperation
Rib cage development, 24, 51, 54 ff.
Routines, exercise:
  abbreviated, 65 ff.
  alternating, 67 ff.
  basic, 64 ff.
Rowing, bent over, 22, 39, 43 ff., 45, 66

Safety, 8, 47 (*see also* Equipment; Injuries; Knee injuries; Spotters; Stretching; Training, frequency; Warming up; Weight selection and progression)
Sandow, Eugen, 55
Schwarzenegger, Arnold, 18, 21, 58, 95
Shoulder development, 22, 27, 38, 41, 42 ff., 53
Sleep, 25, 75 ff., 91, 93
Smith, Charles A., 31
Spotters, 41, 52, 53, 62, 63, 64
Squat:
  breathing (Eells style), 32 ff.

breathing technique, 23 ff., 49 ff.
depth, 47
economic influences on popularity, 17 ff.
form, 47 ff.
(*See also* Belts; Equipment; Safety)
Steinborn, Henry ("Milo"), 28, 29, 33
Strength, 28
Strength goals, 85 ff.
Strength & Health, 34
Stretching, 60
Style, exercise, 58 ff.

Teegarden, Chester O., 80
Thighs, development, 46 ff.
Tornabene, Dean, 19
Training:
  frequency, 66 ff.
  log, 86 ff.
  poundages, 59 ff.

Warming up, 60, ff.
Weight selection and progression, 59 ff.
Willpower, 24
Women, 15
Work, intensity of, 22 ff., 50 ff.

York Barbell Company, 34

About the Author

Randall J. Strossen was introduced to weight training when he was about eight, when one of his uncles brought him to the basement gym where he trained. When he was thirteen, Randall got his first set of weights, a standard 110-pound set. Much to his chagrin, he recalls that it was his diminutive mother who easily carried the whole set from the store to the car.

Several years later, much stronger but not that much bulkier, Randall first used the training program described in this book and gained 30 pounds of muscle in six weeks, progress sufficiently dramatic to be reported in the January 1969 issue of *Iron Man* magazine. Shortly thereafter, Randall was power cleaning 250, squatting 405 for five reps, and deadlifting 495, all drug-free and without wraps —very respectable lifts for a 180-pound seventeen-year old in 1969. He has never forgotten the near-miracle of heavy, 20-rep squats and, following his own advice, he squatted with well over 300 pounds for 20 reps while writing this book.

After earning a Ph.D. in psychology from Stanford University, Randall joined Bank of America, where he first became a vice president of marketing research and planning, and then a vice president of new product development. Four years later he went to Coopers & Lybrand, where he spent three years as a senior consultant, before leaving to become an independent consultant and a free-lance writer. In 1988 Randall formed IronMind™ Enterprises, dedicated to enhancing performance in the strength sports by developing and applying techniques based on scientific psychology. The philosophy at IronMind® Enterprises, Inc. is "Stronger minds, stronger bodies."

Not just a gym rat, Randall has had more than a measure of success in a wide range of sports—from ice hockey to rock climbing to bicycle racing to wrist-wrestling—and has won awards in academia, business, and journalism, as well as athletics. He currently writes the sports psychology column for *IRONMAN* magazine and contributes articles to *Powerlifting USA, IRONSPORT, Weightlifting USA,* and *Hardgainer.*

Additional copies of *Super Squats* are available for $12.95 per copy, plus $2.00 postage and handling, from:

IronMind® Enterprises, Inc.
P.O. Box 1228
Nevada City, CA 95959

For orders of ten or more books, the unit price is $9.95 and we'll pay the postage and handling. Prices subject to change.